African Village Man Kills Lion With A Pencil

African Village Man Kills Lion With A Pencil

Victor Ekworomadu

BOOKLOGIX®
Alpharetta, Georgia

The author has tried to recreate events, locations, and conversations from his/her memories of them. The author has made every effort to give credit to the source of any images, quotes, or other material contained within and obtain permissions when feasible.

Copyright © 2025 by Victor Ekworomadu

All rights reserved. No part of this book may be reproduced or transmitted in any form or by any means, electronic or mechanical, including photocopying, recording, or any information storage and retrieval system, without permission in writing from the author.

ISBN: 978-1-6653-0830-4 - Paperback
eISBN: 978-1-6653-0831-1- eBook

These ISBNs are the property of BookLogix for the express purpose of sales and distribution of this title. The content of this book is the property of the copyright holder only. BookLogix does not hold any ownership of the content of this book and is not liable in any way for the materials contained within. The views and opinions expressed in this book are the property of the Author/Copyright holder, and do not necessarily reflect those of BookLogix.

Library of Congress Control Number: 2024923369

☉This paper meets the requirements of ANSI/NISO Z39.48-1992 (Permanence of Paper)

1 2 0 4 2 4

I want to dedicate this book to my lovely parents.

Mom and Dad

My mom, Adaezeagwula, and my dad, Ekworomadu Oghonna, lived a life of honor, dignity, respect, and love for all people. My mom was the village's pharmacist, producer of local laxative, disciplinarian woman mentor and industrious. She passed away at the age of ninety-three of a broken heart after her younger brother and sister passed away, followed by my older brother—her oldest son—whom she had thought would assist in burying her when her time came.

On the other hand, my dad, a mediator, peacemaker, and a man that held lots of wisdom, died at the age of one hundred from natural causes. As it goes, one's life is not measured by how long he or she lived, but how they lived.

Content

Foreword ix
Acknowledgments xv
Introduction xvii
A Glimpse of Nigeria xix

Part I

Chapter 1: Family 1
Chapter 2: Young Entrepreneur 5
Chapter 3: The High School Days 11
Chapter 4: Welcome to Adulthood 17
Chapter 5: College Life in America 21
Chapter 6: Love and the Workforce 33
Chapter 7: New Life in Dentistry 39
Chapter 8: Baby Fever 51

Gallery 73

Part II

Wisdom from the Nigerian Elders 91
Wisdom Stories 93
Wisdom Words with Interpretation 97

Foreword

When a book about the life and work of one individual lifts up basic truths that connect with some of the experiences of people around the world, that is a good book. Victor Ekworomadu has written such a book. In this moving account of his journey from a village in Nigeria, to where he is now a beloved colleague in an office founded by the legendary Atlanta dentist, Dr. Ronald Goldstein, we are privy to how education transformed Victor Ekworomadu's life. This is an experience many people around the world have had, and unfortunately, too many have been denied.

As I was reading this story of how Victor Ekworomadu overcame adversities to become who he is today, I heard echoes from my own journey as a Black woman who grew up in Jacksonville, Florida, during the era of racial segregation. Many who read this story who are in marginalized communities will also hear echoes from their own lives in terms of the power of faith, the necessity for perseverance, and the importance of collaborating with others to get through challenging times.

This compelling story of how Victor Ekworomadu came to believe that doing for others is just the rent you have to pay for your room on earth will surely resonate with people of diverse backgrounds and identities who also believe being of service to others is a key to living a good and joyful life. The final chapter of this very special book treats us to the wisdom and the joy that Nigerian proverbs can bring into our lives.

—Dr. Johnnetta Betsch Cole, President Emerita of Spelman and Bennett Colleges, Director Emerita of the Smithsonian National Museum of African Art, and President of the National Council of Negro Women.

Victor Ekworomadu is a unique individual whose heart is made of gold. His brain functions on what he can do for others; his proven goal is to make the world a better place to live in.

Victor's humor and laughter are contagious. Born in Nigeria, his life story reads like a movie script! I met Victor thirty years ago when he came to work with our Goldstein, Garber, and Salama Dental Team of forty. We are in the business of making our patients have a better life with their new smiles. Not only did Victor ingratiate himself with all the doctors, patients, and staff, but his work was something to behold. He quickly won our Employee of the Year award so often, we had to change the title to the "Victor Award."

Victor works quickly and effectively, but he is never too busy to be of help to anyone in need. In fact, he started a very successful charity called Hope and Love, which helps former prisoners and the needy. In order to raise money for the charity, he secured items of clothing, appliances, and other things from individuals, then he would hold sales, and give the items to those who were in need.

To show just how creative Victor is, he arranged a reunion of all our former staff members plus another reunion for members of his extended family throughout Nigeria and America to come to Atlanta. And what a reunion it was, complete with African music, dancing, and food!

I have never known Victor to say "No" to anyone. He always finds a way to complete the smallest to the largest of tasks quietly and efficiently. Victor has been in charge of office logistics and he does an amazing job without any requests for help.

Victor has the stuff heroes are made from. He has been a champion for us, plus for the communities he has lived and worked in. After reading his story, I am sure you will agree. Personally, Victor has been a delight to have on our team for over thirty years. He makes each day a happy place to be with his smiles and laughter. And since he loves to be happy, he makes us happy, even on more difficult days when we may have multiple emergencies. He is truly the heart of our office and his humorous stories and sayings are guaranteed to brighten anyone's day.

Victor Ekworomadu is truly a Man for All Seasons and we are all so proud to have his life story for all to read.

—Ronald Goldstein, DDS, Goldstein, Garber, and Salama, is currently Clinical Professor of Restorative Sciences at the Dental College of Georgia, Augusta University, Adjunct Clinical Professor of Prosthodontics at Boston University Henry M. Goldman School of Dental Medicine, Adjunct Professor in the Associated Faculty in the Department of Periodontics at the University of Pennsylvania School of Dental Medicine, and an Adjunct Professor of Restorative Dentistry at the University of Texas Health Science Center at San Antonio, Texas. He is a contributor to ten published texts and Author of the *Text Esthetics in Dentistry*, third edition, published by Wiley in 2018. His best-selling consumer book for the public, entitled *Change Your Smile*, now in its fourth edition, has been read by millions of people and has been translated into twelve languages.

Victor Ekworomadu is a rare and dear friend to us—and to so many others. In this book, Victor shares his compelling story. From his early upbringing in rural Nigeria, West Africa, to his university years in the United States, and ultimately becoming a vital and cherished member of a community in Atlanta, America, Victor's journey is one of profound influence. His presence has significantly enriched the lives of all those around him.

For over three decades, we have worked together successfully at our dental practice, Goldstein, Garber, and Salama, and beyond. Victor has shown an unwavering commitment to integrating and supporting everyone—patients, doctors, staff, and even those in need, whether they be in shelters, homeless, or on the streets. This daily challenge is Victor's commitment, one he approaches with a quiet yet resolute charm, steadfast integrity, and a subtle sense of humor.

Victor is a man of remarkable adaptability, able to navigate different eras and circumstances with ease. He is well-regarded for his impartiality, often serving as the voice of reason, intelligence, and common sense amidst the inevitable complexities of life. His extensive technical knowledge ensures that the physical infrastructure and human relations of our interdisciplinary practice run smoothly. Whether dealing with floods, power cuts, the pandemic, or the daily challenges of life, Victor keeps everything—and everyone—in order.

He is a friend who instinctively recognizes the slightest need in others and discreetly addresses it, whether with a hug, advice, assistance, or simply offering shelter. Beyond the technical and logistical aspects of our practice, Victor has been the pivotal bond that has kept doctors, staff, and patients connected. His organization of routine gatherings, events, and the

Victor Ekworomadu

recent thirty-five-year reunion of past and present personnel has been invaluable.

Victor is that friend in Deed—whenever in Need.

—Doctors David Garber and Maurice Salama are internationally renowned multidisciplinary educators, recognized as "Team Atlanta." They are founding partners of the world's leading dental education website, and are invited as speakers globally. They are clinical researchers and have published an excess of 120 articles in peer reviewed journals and book chapters, as well as co-authored several dental textbooks.

—Dr. David Garber is a Professor in the Department of Periodontics and the Department of Oral Rehabilitation at the University of Augusta, Georgia. He also served as a clinical professor in the Department of Prosthodontics at Louisiana State University and a clinical professor in the Department of Restorative Dentistry at the University of Texas in San Antonio.

—Dr. Maurice Salama is a Clinical Professor in the Department of Periodontics at the University of Augusta, Georgia and with the faculty of the University of Pennsylvania. Dr. Salama has dual specialty training in Periodontics and Orthodontics with additional training in Implant Dentistry at the Branemark Center at the University of Pennsylvania.

Dr. Salama is CEO of the Salama Training Centers in Miami and Romania, which offer yearlong Implant Mastership Residency Programs in the USA and Europe.

Acknowledgments

Before I start to write this story, I want to thank God and my parents, who laid the foundation that molded me to become who I am today and supported me in coming to the United States for my studies. At the same time, I must not fail to thank my other family members, who encouraged me to always focus and work hard. Finally, I thank my employers, coworkers, and friends who stood by me during both the good times and the challenging times. Special thanks to Samuel Ekworomadu, my older brother who came to the United States first and encouraged me to join him.

Thank you to Jennifer Glynn, Dr. Ronald Goldstein, Judy Goldstein, Josephine Ekworomadu, Annette Mathews, Emily McAlvin, David Ekworomadu, Phoebe Han, Ezekiel Ekworomadu, Liz Chisom Ekworomadu, Mr. Bobby Ezor, and Kennedy Ekworomadu. These people also contributed to making this story/book possible.

Our thanks and appreciation to one of the pilots who helped Biafra during the civil war. His name was Johnny from Israel, and he was so good. He saved a lot of lives and was nicknamed Johnny Biafra.

As you read this story, you will discover that it touches on so many areas of my life and experiences, and at the end, you will get a glimpse of my father's and elders' words of wisdom, which guided me in making many important decisions. Enjoy the story.

A majority of the proceeds from this story will go toward supporting Hope and Love Charity for Families of Georgia, a nonprofit 501(c)(3), and was created to assist families in the Metro Atlanta area who are experiencing hard times and assisting with much-needed help to the mini shelters and food banks in and around the city.

Introduction

Everyone has a life story. Sometimes their stories might be similar, sometimes they are very different. This is my life story.

An African village man kills a lion with a pencil. You might wonder, *How in the world did he use a pencil to kill a lion?*

I was the youngest of six children raised by a widowed mother after my father passed away while I was in high school. Thanks to my constant studying, I was appointed to be in charge of the boy's dormitory in a high school of approximately 250 boys, some of them much bigger and older than I. At a young age, I became an entrepreneur to save money while working in Nigeria to put myself through college with no assistance, despite the many challenges, and pursued my higher education in the United States but was only able to come with a few clothes and little money. I knew life would not be easy.

While in college, I received several honor certificates and that was the reason I had to sharpen my pencil to face the aggressive lion. Upon graduating college, I received a plaque of appreciation for service and loyalty from Northridge Country Club in Texas, passed an American citizen test to obtain my citizenship, received performance recognition from the Department of Radiology at North Fulton Regional Hospital in Atlanta, and also received the Employee of the Year Gold Award from Drs. Goldstein, Garber, and Salama LLC in Georgia. After that, I consistently won Employee of the Year for several years among forty-plus employees, and the award was eventually renamed to the "Victor Award" at Goldstein, Garber, and Salama, to give others a chance to win. From Drs. Goldstein, Garber, and Salama, I also received the certificate for being the ideal and outstanding employee. The next certificate I received was the Appreciation for Contribution to the Community Service Department at Mountains of Praise Church in Marietta, and I received another certificate of Appreciation for Outstanding Dedication and Support of the Kennestone Hospital Volunteer Program at Kennestone Regional Healthcare System. I proudly organized and hosted a family reunion in the United States, which brought together many families who'd not seen each other for more than twenty years. I also organized a Goldstein, Garber, and Salama reunion and appreciation event, which brought together so many current and former employees—even those from out of state.

In 2003, my wife and I formed a 501 (c)(3) nonprofit organization, Hope and Love for Families of Georgia, that has helped more than eight hundred families in the state of Georgia, then we adopted a six-month-old boy from Africa.

It is an honor I have for God, my parents, the elders, and those in authority who gave me the audacity and blessing to kill lions with pencils.

If I don't contribute to society, I'll feel like a parasite to the society. Honor is a powerful instrument that can assist in life to achieve our goals, and all it would take is a pencil.

Please read the rest of the story about how the African village man killed a lion with a pencil.

A Glimpse of Nigeria

Nigeria, also known as the Mother of Africa, is located in the Western part of Africa and was ruled by the British until 1960, when Nigeria formally became independent. Nigeria was divided into four regions; northern, eastern, western, and southern, but now has many states and is the most populated country in Africa, with a population of over two hundred million. The most common languages spoken are English, Igbo, Hausa, Yoruba, Efik, and so many other dialects. Nigeria is blessed with so many mineral resources, such as crude oil, natural gas, gold, coal, iron ore, gemstones, bitumen, and barite. The color of the Nigerian flag is green and has white stripes—the green represents agriculture productivity, while the white stripes represent peace and harmony. Nigeria produces lots of Nollywood movies, and the most popular sport there is soccer. In the olden day of Nigeria, you could marry as many wives as you wanted and wouldn't go to jail for it. They did this to expand their families if the first wife was unable to have a child—but the many wives might have given you a bald head.

Nigeria had a bloody civil war that started in 1967. I was eleven years old, and my sister and I were living with my oldest brother, who was a vice principal for a women's training college in Cross River State. I remember hearing the news that everyone should vacate to their home states, and we had to pack all our belongings and head home. As soon as we got there—to my state in the eastern part of Nigeria—I could hear the sounds of rockets in the Umuahia market near my village.

There were many casualties as the war persisted, and the military started to come to villages to draft young men to go fight. I remember my mom always looking out for my brothers, telling them to go and hide. After a couple of months, my four brothers were tired of hiding and, all of a sudden, one of my brothers disappeared for weeks. We couldn't figure out where he went, and we were all crying every day.

He came home one day and told us he'd been in the training camp as a military officer and would be deployed in a couple of days. My mom was so sad but could not prevent him from going, so we all prayed for his safe return. My other two brothers joined the national food directorate to be in charge of distributing food to the military and those in refugee camps, and my last brother joined the research and production unit (the unit responsible for researching, manufacturing, and testing military equipment).

After all my brothers were gone, it was my sister, me, Mom, and Dad at the house. One evening, we heard a rocket explosion not too far from our house. We found out a rocket had hit a house nearby, and it hit a woman living by herself after her husband passed away several years earlier.

On hearing of the death, we packed a few things—we could not carry much since we would be walking on foot—and left. After walking several miles, we came to a big river where the only way to pass through was by boat. My mom refused to go into the boat. We begged her and assured her that we would all be safe, and after forty minutes of negotiations, she finally agreed as long as we held her hands and she kept her eyes closed. Immediately, we crossed to the other side of the river, and we were relieved.

After several miles, it started to get dark. We ended up at a family friend's house, a reverend minister who allowed us to stay with them. We all slept on the floor on a mat we had, and after a couple of days, we told them we would be leaving not to wear out our welcome (the minister had five children). I remember we slept under the tree for a couple of nights.

After a couple more days, we arrived at the refugee center where we settled which happened to be close to where my oldest brother was stationed. He always brought us food, which was a huge blessing, but one day, we heard news that my other brother, the second oldest who joined the military, was shot, and was in the hospital recovering from a bullet wound. From what we heard, he had a grenade on his waist when he was shot—which would have been a different story had the bullet hit the grenade. He survived the gunshot wound and was awarded a promotion to captain.

The three years of fighting between the Nigerian and Biafra militaries led to a lot of starvation and malnutrition among the children. As the war continued, it became obvious that all was lost by Biafra, and Ojukwu was convinced to leave the country to avoid being assassinated.

On January 9, 1970, I was fourteen years old when the Nigeria/Biafra war ended, and people started going back to their various hometowns to start life all over again.

Unfortunately, one of my cousins who joined the military did not return home. I remember after the war, my cousin's mom would come out from her house, crying and calling for her son to come home, and it was so emotional for me to hear that. War is not a good thing. It should be avoided by all means if possible, the negative impact it has on people is beyond comprehension.

Uzoma's Wedding Event

Uzoma is my nephew, his name means "good journey." This is him surrounded by my cousins, nephews, nieces, my mom, sister, and in-laws. He owns and operates his hotel business in Umuahia Abia State. He was the flag bearer representing Accord Political Party.

Nigerian flag

The white color stands for unity and peace, and green for agriculture.

Ekworomadu, Aguocha, and Ezeagwula Family Reunion

Some of our family members have not seen each other for more than twenty years, coming from Atlanta, Dallas, Texas, Houston Texas, Toronto Canada, Little Rock Arkansas, Denver, etc. Dr. Goldstein and Dr. Garber attended as a part of our family. Everyone had a wonderful time.

PART I

● ● ● ● ● ● ●
Chapter 1: Family

My father gave me the name Ulonna, which means "my father's house," and my mother named me Victor Chukwuemeka Ekworomadu. My middle name translates to "God has done great" in Igbo. I was born and raised in eastern Nigeria in the village of Eke-Oba, which is roughly 365 miles from the former Nigeria capital, Lagos, which has since relocated to Abuja. I am the youngest of six children—five boys and one girl. We have a large extended family too! Currently, I have twelve nephews, nine nieces, and over eighty cousins!

My mother was one of the most noted female leaders in the village. She was a strong, industrious, and self-disciplined woman. She was also very spiritual, passionate about volunteering with the church, mentoring women throughout the village, and taking charge of the women's group treasury. In addition to the community, my mother was devoted to taking care of her own family, rising at five every morning for prayer, returning to cook breakfast for the family, and then working on the family farm, often until six in the evening. Not only did she keep herself busy on the farm, in the church, and within the community, but she also managed the village palm oil processing plant and was responsible for the development of laxatives she sold to the people within the village. I always teased her and told her she should have gotten a pharmaceutical license. Even after her long days, she still came home to take care of her children and family.

There were several farms within the community, all of them several miles apart from each other. The farms ranged in size from four to eight acres and produced a mountain of different goods. My mother, with the help of laborers and sometimes my siblings and me, worked on these farms on a daily basis, often on weekends and holidays. We assisted with everything from planting and harvesting the goods for sale. We even got to "sample" the yummy fruits and veggies, making sure they were safe for consumption. These farms produced various kinds of vegetables, peanuts, yams, cassava, peppers, and all kinds of tropical fruits, while other farms raised chickens and produced palm oils and palm wines. Thanks to the hard work my mother put in, we rarely went to the markets for food with the exception of salt, sugar, and other seasonings. As a matter of fact, my mom was nicknamed Ada Okpokoro Achara, because she always produced or harvested the biggest Achara vegetable in the entire village, the Okpokoro Achara. Achara is a vegetable in the celery family, and Ada means the oldest daughter in the family, referencing to the big fruit. My mom definitely had a green thumb.

My mother had a heart for the community and would go out

of her way to make sure other families had food and the necessities they needed to survive. She would take them to our family farm and bless them with food if they were without. These values were taught to all of us at a young age with very specific guidelines we were expected to live by:

- ✗ Do not accept any food from a stranger.
- ✗ Do not associate with someone with questionable character.
- ✗ Do not associate with or be intimate with the opposite sex until you're finished with school and are married.
- ✗ Be home by six p.m. every day and do not lie around the outside of the house.

If there was ever a dispute among the siblings, she would leave it up to us to settle the problem and would not accept any gifts from the children until the dispute was settled.

When it came to discipline, my mother was known for her rigidness. I recall a time when I was twelve years old and my oldest brother had invited a schoolmate over during the summer. The schoolmate was what was called "a day lady"—she had come over during the day to "discuss school work" and "study" with my brother. The hours passed, and she was still hanging out in the house with my brother, and near supper time my mother clearly had enough of his behavior. She marched into his room and questioned his company, making her go home. My brother was quite embarrassed about this. He went on a "hunger strike" that day as he tried to get over his embarrassment.

Despite my mother's seemingly disciplined demeanor, I adored her. She had loved the community and was committed to nurturing the villagers. It was obvious to all that would meet her.

I would follow her everywhere because I looked up to her and always wanted to be by her side. Even when she would make trips to the market out of the village, I would want to be with her. She always joked around with me that she was going to end up moving in with me when I went away to college, which I thought was a great but funny idea at the time.

My father was also well-known in the village. He was a well-respected village elder and full of wisdom and knowledge. People always came to him to settle disputes ranging from disagreements about land or questions regarding loans. The villagers looked up to him for his fair and diplomatic decision-making. Before beginning any case, he would start with words of wisdom, which would usually ease tension between the bickering parties to reduce the name-calling and finger-pointing. His two favorite proverbs were "you reap what you sow" and "don't take shortcuts in life." Another one of his philosophies was to "always keep your hands clean in life, no matter what you are doing." My father was a quiet man, packed with wisdom. His words of wisdom have impacted my life in so many ways today. He would be proud of the man I have become and the family I have raised, but sadly he passed away while I was in high school. He has been greatly missed.

I remember, growing up in the village, there wasn't much in the way of entertainment. Village life revolved around church, school, work, and family. Occasionally I would join the other groups of children and play soccer in the fields, and I also sang in the church choir. Our mission trips through the church involved more outdoor activities and volunteering on the farm in one-hundred-degree weather. No wonder I have a permanent suntan!

●●●●●●●

Chapter 2: Young Entrepreneur

Growing up as the youngest child in the family, I never wanted to be spoiled or coddled, but instead wanted to be independent. I admired my parents and their hard work and wanted to be respectful, independent, and helpful like them. I was raised to respect my elders as well as all authority figures, knowing I would fit into one or both of those groups one day. By the time I was about eight years old, I knew I wanted to be a business professional. I started saving money I earned from helping the people of my village with small tasks. Often, I would run errands for elderly neighbors, and help them push their bikes through the hills. A one-way savings box was created for me to deposit my earnings so I could not take the money out of it. In an effort to multiply my hard-earned money, I devised a plan and decided to purchase a chicken with my savings. I bought the chicken and she laid eight eggs, six of them hatching to chicks. At that point, I sold the six chicks and came up with enough money to buy bread and kerosene to sell in the village. You may be asking, "Why kerosene?" In my village, electricity was not consistent and often went out for a couple of days at a time. When the power went out, we had to rely on kerosene lanterns. The business, which I ran in my spare time after school, was a success and benefited the people in the village.

I learned so many important lessons as a young entrepreneur. One of the most important lessons I learned in business was the value of location. Like they say, "location, location, location." Whoever started saying this knew what they were talking about. While I was selling bread and kerosene in the village, my brother suggested we invent a kiosk. This was a great idea because I was worn out from selling bread in the hot Nigerian sun all afternoon! My brother and I split the cost of purchasing the kiosk and he supplied the goods to fill it. We set up the kiosk outside the Holy Rosary Girl's Secondary School in the township and filled the kiosk with the usual: kerosene, sugar, soft drinks, matches, toothbrushes, toothpaste, powder, aspirin, bottled water, lotion, soap, bread, etc. The bread was a special kind I was not familiar with, called "women's bread," and it was a big seller outside this all-girls school. We had picked a great location to set up work, and everything sold well, but the "women's bread" sold like hotcakes and we struggled to keep them in stock.

In my young age, I was naively unaware of what "women's bread" was and what it was used for. It sure was popular with the pretty girls at the school and they were often shy about purchasing this product and would ask me to wrap the bread for them to hide it from their boyfriends. I could not for the life of me figure out what it was! I finally asked one of the young ladies what the women's bread was used for and why only girls bought it. She stared at me for a few minutes and I thought I had asked a very naughty question. I nervously asked her again and she responded to me by asking me if I had a sister. I told her, "Yes, I have a sister." The young lady told me to go home and ask my sister what the "women's bread" was used for before I embarrassed myself some more. Well, I was not expecting that answer. I went home that afternoon and asked my sister and got an answer I was totally not expecting. Apparently, I had been selling feminine hygiene products through my kiosk! No wonder my brother suggested setting up the kiosk next to the all-girls school. It was a brilliant idea and a great location!

With the success of the business, I decided to take things to the next level. During the long summer break from school, I traveled to the larger town, Umuahia, outside of the village and went to the bakeries there. I would buy between one and two hundred loaves of bread from the bakery and start selling it on the street. Business was once again a success!

I sold out of bread early one day and decided to travel to a few different bakeries to buy more bread, but they were all sold out. Luckily—or maybe unluckily—I found a bakery that still had bread and bought another hundred loaves. The bakery was called "Angie's Bakery" and was owned and run by a nice lady named Angie.

The hours passed by on the street, but the bread was not selling, and people were questioning where I got the bread from. They would either see the label or I would tell them I got it from Angie's Bakery. It turned out that people did not want to buy her bread simply because she had lived a questionable lifestyle in previous years and they worried she might have touched the bread, making it unclean. I think this was just a traditional mindset, but I thought it was rather silly. The entrepreneur's former profession, despite the villagers' disapproval of it, did not matter to me. However, I was about to be out of business because of it! I was getting nervous, but a brilliant thought hit me. I ended up removing Angie's label from the bread and was able to sell the remaining loaves. This idea and event taught me my first bit of "business wisdom."

Umuahia Township

This is where I was selling bread on the street both in the residential area and in the market. One day, it occurred to me I could sell more bread at the train station, though you had to have a permit to sell at this location. I usually took only a few loaves of bread to sell at the train station so it would be easier for me to run if they caught me selling without a permit. One day I nearly got caught! I ran so fast like lightning and I have never gone back to that train station.

This is the commercial section of Umuahia where I sold most of my bread trying to get rich.

Umuhu Central School

This is where I attended elementary school. The motto is hard work and progress. I believe, if you work hard in life, there is no doubt you will not progress and achieve your goal. It was about three miles to walk to school from our house.

Chapter 3: The High School Days

My business affairs in town were tough enough, but school posed an entirely different set of challenges for me. During my elementary school days, we walked several miles to and from school. Discipline was the norm, so if you misbehaved for any reason, the teacher would discipline you, then you would go home and receive more discipline from your parents.

Every Monday, the teacher would go around the classroom and check the hygiene of each student, focusing on your hair, teeth, nails, and clothes. If anything was out of place, you would be punished and sent home. Morning meetings in the chapel were mandatory for every student. We would sing gospel songs and pray before starting class each day. There was absolutely no tolerance for disrespect or disobedience by the students.

I remember an incident from those days in which I managed to get myself in trouble. It was Good Friday and a couple of friends and I were playing in the schoolyard. We came across a mango tree growing in the yard, and we picked a few and ate them. Picking and consuming the fruit growing in the yard was against school rules and was punishable, and apparently, someone saw us and wrote us up. Our names were called to the chapel during the morning service in front of everyone, and our punishment for eating the fruit was to uproot a tree with a shovel and we weren't allowed to attend any classes until the job was done.

My high school was also centered around discipline. While I was in high school, I was living on campus in a highly disciplined and structured dormitory. The stipulation was that there was to be absolutely no outside activity interfering with education and school. We woke up every morning around five and got ready for the day—we had to make our beds and tidy our living area in the dormitory before heading to the chapel for prayers and to sing. There were about one thousand students, both boys and girls, and there were four housing dorms for all of the boys and four for the girls. The Boarding House Masters were very strict, they would ring the bell to let us know it was time to eat, and if we ran late, we would miss that meal. The dining room doors would close and lock and our food would be thrown away. Once the mealtime was over, we cleared our plates, whether we were done eating or not. There was a designated time for class and time for prayer services and we were expected to attend them both as they were scheduled or face punishment.

If we were caught loitering around the campus or walking the halls when we were supposed to be in class, we would be punished. One of the most common punishments was to fetch ten to fifteen buckets of water for the school cooks, from the stream where we would get our water about five miles from the school, which, of course, we walked. The level of discipline and the school made me think I was in a military school. However the structure, discipline, and hard work my school and my parents instilled in me have helped me throughout my life's journey.

One of the most embarrassing moments in my life occurred during my high school days. During my junior year, I was appointed as the house prefect for house B which housed about 250 students. My job as the house prefect was to take charge of the students' activities, inspect the house every weekend, and make sure the students made it to class, sports, and chapel on time. Another duty of mine was to represent the house and organize a farewell party for my predecessor, who was the house prefect before me and was graduating and leaving the school. Every house prefect had to do the same. The send-off was to be done in the chapel with all the students, teachers, and honored guests and it was my responsibility to read off a farewell speech and acknowledge all the progress, leadership, and achievements of my predecessor and our dormitory.

I was never a good public speaker, so this terrified me. The night before the send-off day celebration, I read through the speech I had written and was starting to get nervous. Throughout my childhood, I was a rather shy guy, yet here I was about to read a speech in front of the entire student body. On the day of the celebration, I was a nervous wreck. I asked the other four house prefects to share their speeches before me so I would have time to compose myself. When it was time for me to present my own speech, I started shaking like a leaf from being so nervous, and the sweat began to pour out of me. My clothes were soaked with sweat, and my hands were clammy and would not stop shaking. I stood there in front of the students, at the head of the chapel, and I just froze. The words were stuck in my mouth as if I were eating a jar of peanut butter. I ended up handing my speech over to another student to read it for me. It took weeks to get over the embarrassment of this event, but the good news was that at the end of the semester, my house won two trophies, one in sports and another in drama.

The events at school and my upbringing at home shaped me into the man I am today. It distinguished some strong characteristics as well as likes and dislikes. I appreciate good people who are beautiful on the inside (and the outside) and who are respectful, genuine, organized, honest, humorous, and caring. I like a beautiful smile that shines into the soul and demonstrates joy and happiness. I enjoy some of the simpler things in life like good (and healthy) food, soft music, gospel, the occasional vacation at the beach, and my favorite delicacy, fried zebra. Just kidding, I don't eat zebras—but I do like to eat nuts, just not too many. I would rather not be identified as being "nutty." I also learned spring and fall are my favorite times of the year—not too hot, not too cold—soccer and tennis are my favorite sports, and my favorite color is light blue. I admire organization, positivity, honesty, appreciation, and love all people. After growing up in Nigeria and traveling to the US, I can safely say I have a strong dislike for cold weather.

This is my high school picture modeling pose.

Evangel High School Abia State Nigeria

Evangel High School was founded by a handful of visionaries within the leadership of Assemblies of God in 1962, two years after Nigerian Independence and the civil war in 1970. The fathers swung into action to rebuild the school that was severely damaged during the war. My oldest brother was the vice principal and several of my family members attended this school.

At Evangel High School, we search for knowledge, truth, and we seek God who guides us always. When life is over, we meet our Maker who will say well done.

● ● ● ● ● ● ●
Chapter 4: Welcome to Adulthood

The time passed and I graduated from high school at around sixteen years old. My goal was to attend college and hopefully become a businessman, but before I entered college, I began teaching kindergarten children. In Nigeria, they call it auxiliary teaching, but here in the US, they call it substitute teaching. I remember we were paid every month with cash. They put your pay in a brown envelope with holes—I still don't know why the envelope has to have holes, maybe so the cash wouldn't suffocate! I was very excited to receive my pay cash. When I received my first pay, I spread the cash on the table and then divided it into three. I don't remember how much it was, but I allocated a portion to my dad, another portion to my mom, and the last portion I paid myself—which I used some of it to buy a turntable and some records. I did not plan to be a rock star because I didn't have long hair, I just loved to listen to music!

This opportunity gave me time to study for some advanced exams known as the General Certificate of Education, or GCE. With this knowledge and training under my belt, one of my older brothers wanted me to interview with one of his friends who oversaw the Federal Forestry Reserve, which was managed by the federal government in Nigeria. If you are selected for the position, the government will send you to a two-year training program with fair pay and great benefits. I was thrilled and felt as though God had buttered my bread! The first and second interviews went great and I waited with confidence for the orientation to finalize. Unfortunately, I got a disappointing letter letting me know I was not selected for the position. I felt as though my whole world had crumbled. My buttered bread had been eaten by someone else! My brother and I could not figure out what went wrong, and we later got the unfortunate news that someone else was competing for the position and successfully bribed the director to give him the job. My brother and I were raised with more morals and did not believe in bribery because it encourages corruption. This brings me to another one of my father's proverbs: "Whatever you are doing, keep your hands clean so you don't have to watch your back."

Since this opportunity did not work out as expected, I went back to auxiliary teaching, which was over three hundred miles from my house. I wanted to be independent and not burden my family, so I needed to consider a more permanent line of work as well as figure out steady transportation arrangements. After a couple of months, my brother in Lagos reached out to me while he was working with the Exxon Mobile Oil Production Company. He introduced me to one of his friends who was working for the Nigerian Reinsurance Corporation and was able to give me a good reference to the editor of the National Publishing Company.

The Publication Company was known as *The Daily Times of Nigerians Limited*. I was interviewed by the editor and hired! They put me in the marketing department to be in charge of overseeing the subscription deck. I was not aware management was watching my performance and monetary accountability. Within a few months, they promoted me to the head of the branch at the international airport. This came as a huge blessing, for the promotion came with a bunch of benefits including travel allowance, an enjoyable work atmosphere, and the opportunity to meet many great people, local and international.

My plan changed after a few years, and I decided I wanted to focus more on the transportation business. I had an idea about purchasing a bus to assist in the transportation of people from place to place. Not everyone had cars, and although there was public transportation in densely populated cities like Lagos, it was lagging in smaller villages.

Once again, my plans changed and I was contacted by my brother, Samuel, in the US. He was studying abroad and invited me to join him in the States. I applied to colleges all over the country: Texas, Arkansas, Washington, and New Jersey—New Jersey and Washington were immediately eliminated upon researching the weather there. Before I could officially be accepted to any of the schools, I had to take the TOEFL exam, which stands for Test of English as a Foreign Language. After passing the exam, I decided to attend school in Little Rock, Arkansas, Philander Smith College (now University). For one thing, the weather there was much warmer than New Jersey and Washington, but I would also be closer to my brother who was also living in Arkansas at the time. It was great being so close to my brother upon moving to a new country where I did not know a single soul!

I planned on flying to the US with my brother the next time he came to see me in Lagos so we could fly back together. When he arrived, we found ourselves scrambling to obtain visas and buy plane tickets and I was unsure if we were going to make the deadline, for we still needed to have everything done in time to be at the airport by six p.m. to catch our flights by nine that evening! We were in such a rush to catch our flight, I failed to return to the village to say goodbye to my mother and the rest of my family. Everything happened so fast, I was also unable to give adequate notice to my employer. To this day, I still regret not being able to do so.

The flight took off at about ten at night. We had a layover in France and from there we flew to Boston, Massachusetts, where it was winter. I saw a bunch of white fluff on the ground outside the window at the airport and my first thought was that it had to be salt. I forgot my geography about snow and I thought to myself, *They are wasting an awful lot of salt*. My brother turned to me and told me it was snow, not salt. Growing up in Nigeria, I had only *heard* about snow, and I thought snow was giant white stones that fell from the sky. Had Google been around in the '80s, I would have quickly discovered exactly what I was looking at.

Besides seeing my first real taste of winter, I saw American freedom and opportunity. And although my parents were not physically there with me on this new journey, I could feel their presence. The lessons they had taught me throughout my life were firmly embedded in me. Honesty, integrity, discipline, respect, and genuine love for others was my way of life, whether in America or Africa, and I was going to stick to that code of ethics regardless of my circumstances. I was to be safe and truthful and avoid any kind of reckless or extravagant behavior while living in America—it was important to me to do what was right, even when nobody was watching.

● ● ● ● ● ● ●
Chapter 5: College Life in America

It was so cold when the plane finally landed in Arkansas. I was absolutely miserable and starting to worry about how I was going to adjust to the drastic climate change. By the time I arrived, classes for the semester had already begun. Even though I registered late, I knew I had to keep ahead of my studies and remain optimistic and determined. Also, it was very important to avoid the distractions that came with college life, such as materialism and girls. I was on a mission and had to remind myself, "I am here for my studies." This proved to be a challenge, for I discovered rather quickly where the values of my classmates were.

I went to class wearing my suit jacket and carrying a briefcase and noticed my female classmates staring and winking at me. I did not know what to think of this or how to react. I found that other schoolmates were using their school fees and financial aid refunds to purchase nice cars and clothes the girls really liked. My brother suggested going to a local dealership and picking out a nice car, but I did not want to indulge in anything that would distract me from my studies. I was attending class to get a valuable education, not to impress girls or gain popularity.

A funny story that justified my thoughts: One day, some of the guys and I called a few of the ladies over at the dormitory. One of the first things the girls had asked us (myself included) was what kind of car we drove. I purposely said that I drove a Pinto, and the girl laughed and told me that it was a piece of junk, but I told her, "It has four wheels and it drives." This confirmed that the primary interest of the ladies was contrary to my own interest, which gave me even more incentive to focus on my studies.

I worked continuously at a full-time job throughout my college days. My first job in America was at the Hilton Hotel and Resort in Little Rock. I went to the interview and applied for the dishwasher position. The interview was short and brief, and the interviewer asked if I could start the job the next day. I was excited about the prospect of independence and earning a living, but unsure at the same time as to what I was getting myself into. I weighed out my options and decided immediately I needed money to fund my stay in college as well as for a car and other expenses. Income equals independence, so I accepted the offer.

I spent the first half of the day at the library on the day my first shift at the Hilton was supposed to start because I had so much homework and the assignments kept piling up! By two o'clock, I finished what I could and caught the next bus into town to start my shift. Upon my arrival, a wedding with nearly two hundred guests was already underway. Wouldn't you know it, I was the only dishwasher at the resort that day. The wait staff kept bringing me piles of dirty dishes and glasses, it was nearly as overwhelming as all the homework I had! It was a mess! I called my brother to come pick me up and he drove right by me, not even recognizing me. Once he picked me up, we discussed my first day at work on the way home. I struggled with the idea of going back to this job because it absorbed every ounce of energy out of me, and I really needed to focus more on my studies. He convinced me to go back for at least one more shift so that adequate notice could be put in but to start looking for a different job. That is exactly what I did and I never regretted it—when one door closes, another one opens.

After saving some money from my dishwashing job, my brother and I started to look for a used car. Every time we called for a car in an ad, we were told the car had already been sold, so when we called an owner and he said, "It is available," we immediately went to see the car. We negotiated the price, and finally, he agreed to accept $550 cash.

We paid him, without even test-driving the car. I don't know what we were thinking. The owner stipulated the car be sold as it is. After we paid him and were about to drive the car, we noticed the steering was so stiff and hard. As a matter of fact, you'd have to eat five to eight fast food burgers or five pounds of fufu to drive the car! (Fufu is an eastern Nigerian food made from cassava or yam powder and it is like a dough. It is eaten with okra or melon seed vegetable soup. The way you eat it is to dip the dough into the soup and throw it into your mouth like you are playing soccer. When you eat fufu, it gives you enough energy to run a marathon. I always made sure I ate fufu before driving the car.)

Not only was the steering so hard but there were also holes all around the body of the car. It was later when I realized the holes were bullet holes. No wonder. When I drove it, the police were staring at the car. I was wondering why they were looking at the car, afraid they thought I didn't buy it with my hard-earned dishwashing money. I think after a year or so, I sold the car so I wouldn't develop a heart problem.

I sold it for the same amount I bought it: $550. Not bad for a grown-up young entrepreneur. Then I bought another used car. This time, it was a Ford Mustang II—which liked to go to the service shop every month. I did not let all the challenges deter me from focusing on my schoolwork.

The next door opened with a position at a country club weeks later. This job was more compatible with my school schedule and my manager and the staff were kind to me, but the job did have one big disadvantage. This country club was not close by and the commute proved to be a challenge at times. One autumn day, I drove myself to work in my little, old second-generation Ford Mustang. Despite it being fall, salt was falling from the sky again! Another "LOL" moment for me—it was snowing again. Had I bothered to check the weather forecast that morning, I would have known to bring a coat and wear something other than my sneakers. After my shift ended that day, I headed home in my Mustang, which did not handle well in snowy and icy conditions. I went to the top of a hill and my car stalled—it would not budge! I got out of the car and could not see anyone for miles. At this point, I was starting to get nervous. The snow was falling and I had to get home. I ended up having to abandon my car and walk several blocks to a pay phone where I was able to reach my brother in the city. When he answered, I told him my situation and asked if he could come pick me up. He was living in a large apartment complex with nearly three hundred residents at the time, and unfortunately one of those residents had parked behind him, blocking him into his spot. In a complex that large, there was no way to locate the owner. At this point, the salt—I mean snow—was four inches deep and was still falling all around me. I tried to call a cab to pick me up, but the line was busy. While I was trying to reach a different taxi service, I saw a bus drive by. I did not know or care where it was going, but I hopped on. Thankfully, it was heading to downtown Little Rock, about five miles from my apartment. This was better than nothing, so I rode the bus downtown and walked the other five miles in the snow, with no coat and just my old sneakers. This was one of my earliest and most miserable experiences about life in America.

Coming to America was a culture shock—not only was the cold weather during the winter season miserable, but when it came to my thick accent, people found it hard to understand me. I sometimes had to say my sentences two to three times before they were able to understand what I was saying. Being in the South, I joked that, maybe if I consumed a lot of grits, black-eyed peas, cornbread, collard greens, peaches, and peanuts, my accent would improve!

Another challenge was the slang. In the early days of living in Little Rock, I first heard someone say, "pay under the table," I thought I had to crawl under the table to get my paycheck. Another one was "gold digger," which I thought meant someone who was literally digging the ground for gold. "Real estate broker" had to be a real estate agent who was broke; "air head" was someone who had actual air in their head; "helicopter parents" were parents who flew helicopters above their kids' heads; "sugar daddy" and "sugar mommy" were parents who sold sugar; and "stepmom" and "stepdad" were parents who had stairs in their house. Even more confusing were phrases such as, "spoiled, rotten kids"—I thought only food could be spoiled and rotten! "Pulling the bull by the horns"—I thought, *You must be crazy to pull a bull by the horns! Unless they were dead or sleeping.* Another phrase was "raining cats and dogs"—what did cats and dogs have to do with the rain?

The one that really got my attention was "money talk." There was a time I didn't have enough money for all my bills, and I quickly remembered the "money talk" phrase. I spread out a few dollar bills on the table and asked them to tell me where all their siblings were—I knew there were thousands of them so where were they!

One day, at the grocery store, I had another culture shock. I was in the produce section, buying some fruits and vegetables, when a beautiful young lady winked at me. I thought maybe something had gotten into her eye or eyelash. I didn't know what it meant, so I looked away. Later, at lunch with my fellow staff members who were all Americans, we were discussing the meaning of these different slangs. I brought up the eye winking, and two of the guys immediately asked me which grocery store I had been at and what I did when the lady winked at me. I told them I did nothing, and just continued shopping, and only then did they explain what it meant. Now, if any lady winks at me with one eye, I wink back with two! Just kidding . . . so I don't end up in the doghouse!

Several months later, I was still working at the Country Club and taking classes. I had a hefty school load at the time and my manager was very kind and understanding, he allowed me to break up my work schedule and work around school. I would usually start work at seven in the morning, leave for classes around nine thirty, which went until about twelve thirty, come back to work, and then leave when my shift was done at around three thirty. After work, I would head over to the library to study and work on my assignments.

One day, I was exhausted from staying up late studying but had to go back to work, struggling to keep my eyes open. I decided to take a quick nap in the janitor's closet and you could just imagine what happened; my brief twenty-minute snooze turned into an amazing two-hour nap! Everyone was looking for me, they thought maybe I had been kidnapped or something and were tempted to call the cops because they knew it was not normal for me to disappear like that. The last place anyone thought to check was the janitor's closet so, naturally, I slept through all of the action. When I woke from my slumber, I stepped out and rubbed my tired red eyes. There was a concerned crowd growing outside the closet, but their concern quickly turned to joy when they realized I had not been kidnapped.

My manager was among them. I was truthful and explained myself to him, and my manager and the rest of the crew were very gracious toward me. They understood and appreciated my struggle to balance my academics and my job. As my mother always told me, hard work never killed anybody. She also said that persistence and determination are the key to unlocking your success. As a result of my good study habits and my high GPA, I was happy to graduate with honors, despite working through college.

Another job I acquired while working my way through college was at Shoney's restaurant with my nephew. We worked the night shift and our responsibility was to clean the restaurant from top to bottom so the place was spotless when patrons returned in the morning. Our shift would start around eight in the evening and go through the night and into the opening hours, usually close to seven a.m. The manager would give us our duties and instructions and lock us in the restaurant to complete the task at hand. Thank God there was never a fire, we had no clue what we would have done! Shoney's would have been serving some *very* crispy toast in the morning! There was never a fire or a life-threatening emergency, and the work was not difficult, which was a good thing.

But unfortunately, my marketing class started at eight a.m. Upon finishing my shift, I would have to rush to the apartment, shower, and head straight to class—there wasn't even time for a crispy toast before class started! I would show up to class at 8:20 every day, with class already well underway and I would miss valuable parts of the lesson. This was my norm, and not a good way to start the day. One day, one of my senior classmates approached me with a little pep talk and encouraged me to adjust my schedule so I could get to class on time. He went on to explain to me that one of the marketing professors was a former police officer, and he frowned upon tardiness of any kind. My classmate, as well as the professor, did not want to see me fail the class. I was so appreciative of this honest advice, I ended up quitting the restaurant within a couple of weeks and managed to make it on time to class for the rest of the semester and pass! New opportunities always come knocking when you close one door.

Upon graduation, I decided to take more advanced classes to further my education. A classmate and I did some research and determined we wanted to continue our education at East Texas State (now known as Texas A&M). The school was about a three-hour drive from Little Rock, so my friend and I decided to take a weekend trip to check out the community. Upon arrival, we immediately liked what we saw and found that the cost of living was reasonable. Further searching led us to find a nice two-bedroom apartment, where the rent was a mere $278 a month. We immediately put down a deposit on the apartment and made our way back to Little Rock to pack up our belongings with the plan being to eventually move back to Little Rock once we finished our courses. I remember tying our mattresses and box springs to the roofs of our car and driving down the highway with one hand on the wheel and the other on our beds. This was a scene straight out of *Driving Miss Daisy*!

When we first arrived in Texas, we called the utility companies to connect our power and water. Despite the lower cost of living, the downside to Texarkana, Texas, was that we discovered the school fees were much higher because we were considered out-of-state applicants. In order for us to be considered in-state applicants, we had to take at least one class in-state prior to applying. I found a junior college nearby, so I took a tennis class there while my roommate took a weightlifting class. We were hoping to be the next Andre Agassi and Sylvester Stallone. The plan worked and we were able to transfer our credits from Arkansas to Texarkana, Texas, and pay both utilities and tuition.

With all of our utilities connected and registration complete, I seriously needed to get another job. The bills were piling up and there was no money coming in. My friend was very fortunate he was able to transfer his job from Little Rock to Texarkana, Texas, but I was not so lucky. I had to find a way to support myself further, so I got a full-time job working at McDonald's, working from four in the morning until noon. That meant getting up at around two or three every morning to go to work, which was a tough adjustment. Even worse, my supervisor was not the most pleasant of individuals and didn't smile much. She hardly acknowledged my presence most of the time, making her quite unapproachable. My father always told me, "Look at a child's face before you accept food from him/her." I tried hard to read into my supervisor and get on her good side, but I just could not figure her out, I could not figure out why she hated life so much. Not once did she ever ask me how school was going or try to even get to know me. Another thing my father told me when I was young was, "Human beings are difficult to deal with." Well, that's no joke. Just when I was done trying to figure her out, I discovered she actually liked and appreciated my hard work as an employee. Who knew?

I had to keep reminding myself this was just the journey, not the destination. Nobody ever said this was going to be an easy breezy adjustment, and overall, the job was not terrible. At least I was making money and the bills were getting paid. My schedule allowed me to get out of work at a decent time to take a nap and spend time at the library studying.

As planned, I returned to Little Rock after finishing my classes in Texarkana, Texas. I really like Arkansas and wanted to settle down there, if only I could find a job. I applied everywhere and attended several interviews, but nothing would materialize. I was being told by the hiring managers I did not have enough experience. The doors were closing on me before I could even get my foot in, but I was determined not to give up.

One day, I ran into Mr. Walter, who was a member of the Little Rock Country Club I worked at before moving to Texas. He was always such a kind gentleman and recognized my hard work. He always gave me tip money for gas and books and always encouraged me. I had given Mr. Walter African artwork as a gift I got when visiting my family in Nigeria, and it really left an impression on him, so we always had a good relationship.

He suggested I open up a boutique and try selling African goods, and that he would even help me get the business going and assist me with the loan process. It seemed like a really good idea, but there just was not enough of a market in Little Rock to keep a business like that afloat. Plus, there was not a lot of tourism or open-minded people who would encourage a business like that. So after considering his words, I continued my job search, which ended up taking me out of Arkansas.

College

This is my college picture. Trying to grow a mustache.

African Village Man Kills Lion with a Pencil

Little Rock, Arkansas

Philander Smith University was formerly known as Philander Smith College in Little Rock, Arkansas. This was where I went to college.

Chapter 6: Love and the Workforce

After my education, I initially wanted to settle in Little Rock, but as I mentioned, there were very few job opportunities there. I applied for so many jobs, and they kept slamming the door in my face for lack of experience, despite a good GPA and excellent references. I decided to move to Atlanta, Georgia, where there was ample work and the cost of living was still reasonable. I worked with several employment agencies, including as an overnight security guard in a trailer at a construction site and warehouse to get some money for my bills, so I didn't have to stand on the street corner with a sign that said, "I will dance for food." I had no gun, knife, or even a slingshot—at least I would have done what David did to Goliath with a slingshot! Thank God I wasn't attacked, I would have been a dead turkey.

I was living in College Park when one day I saw an ad in the paper for a position at a food production company, so I applied. The job offered a nice and consistent seven to three thirty schedule, so I was content there. Unfortunately, after just a couple of months, the plants closed and went out of business, so I was out of a job and back to square one.

Another opportunity came about, and I ended up moving to Norcross, Georgia, in the suburbs just northeast of Atlanta. The rent was reasonable, $350 a month, so I signed a two-year lease. These days, you can hardly rent a storage unit for that cheap! I saw another job opening for an accounting and bookkeeping position at an insurance company in downtown Atlanta, applied for the position, and participated in an interview. The lady conducting the interview seemed impressed and even escorted me to the elevator and said I would hear from her in a few days. However, days and weeks went by, so I called the company and was told that the position had already been filled and I was overlooked due to lack of experience. I didn't even get a chance to prove myself to this company or gain that experience for the future.

This rejection was frustrating, but it did not stop me. I considered going back to school and furthering my education. I looked at a degree working in a pharmacy, but when I applied to Mercer University in Tucker, Georgia, I was told my degree would take an additional three years to achieve, which was too long because I understood it would take longer since I would have to take more college arts and science classes. Instead of college, I decided to volunteer at Dunwoody Medical Center and Kennestone Hospital. I was assigned to the radiography department to assist in all aspects of radiology services. I really enjoyed this and after one year, I was offered a job at North Fulton Hospital in Alpharetta as a radiology assistant.

During my thirties, my family had been pressuring me about settling down and getting married. While I was volunteering at the hospital, some of the ladies asked me if I was married or single. I explained I was single, searching for a very special lady who would meet my specific requirements. I went home that night to work on a list describing my dream woman: She had to be a smart, God-fearing, industrious, passionate, fun, and peaceful woman who could also cook. She also had to be neat and tidy twenty-four/seven. The ladies were eager to hear my list, and when I told them, they did not think I was serious. They asked, "Where in the world are you going to find a woman to meet all of those criteria?" I told myself if I could not find a woman to meet these requirements, I would just quit my day job and become a priest.

One day I was washing my car in front of my apartment, and a young lady approached me and introduced herself to me. Her name was Josephine and she told me she just moved there from New Jersey and did not have any family or friends in Atlanta. I did not have an agenda at the time and just wanted to help, so I told her to let me know if she needed help with anything or information about the area. Apparently, she was living in the same neighborhood as me, and I did not realize it. I eventually noticed her peeking out her window while I was parking my car in a nearby lot, and one day she invited me over for tea, and I accepted her offer. To repay her for her kindness, I offered to take her out to Red Lobster for dinner the next day. She was nice, but I was trying not to get attached because, at that moment, I was planning on moving back to Africa when I was ready. A few days later, despite my reservations, I invited her over for dinner and I cooked an authentic African dish, which she said she enjoyed.

Not only did I win over Josephine with my great cooking, but

I also impressed her with how organized and neat my apartment was. Not to toot my own horn, but I kept it clean and decorated my place with fresh plants and beautiful blooming flowers. She saw all this and asked if a woman was living with me and if I had any kids. I told her, "In fact, I have ten kids in Africa and the woman who lives with me is at work." She understood the joke when I started giggling and we both had a good laugh. Breaking the ice with laughter made us both feel more comfortable, and we were able to enjoy a lovely evening.

But with my move to Africa still in the back of my mind, I went to visit for a few weeks. I was missing home and family and wanted to be with them for a while. Upon my arrival back home to Atlanta, I got extremely sick, and Josephine had to drive me to the hospital. The doctors ran several tests but could not figure out what was wrong. Eventually, they determined I had chickenpox, which is a very serious illness for adults. During my time in the hospital, Josephine came by and ensured the nurses were taking good care of me and after two weeks in the hospital, I was released, and our relationship and friendship continued to grow. I knew I was ready to settle down soon and wanted someone in my life who made it complete. In the meantime, I went back to volunteering at the hospital as a means of giving back to the people who took such good care of me while I was sick.

After two years, I had decided against moving back to Africa, for our relationship had blossomed. The pressure was higher than ever to get married, so we got engaged, and then in August of 1993, we married at the King and Queen Buildings in Sandy Springs. In the presence of our family and friends, we celebrated our happiness. It was a beautiful day.

Victor and Josephine's Wedding

The wedding took place at the King and Queen Building in Sandy Springs, Georgia. It was a happy occasion, celebrated with friends and families. Not only was I waving to the guest, I was waving goodbye to my bachelorhood.

●●●●●●●

Chapter 7: New Life in Dentistry

I continued working at the hospital in North Fulton, but this was proving to be a challenge, especially for us being newlyweds. I was working twelve-hour days, holidays, and weekends, and my time away from home was taking a toll on my marriage. In 1994, I was offered a position at a world-renowned cosmetic dental office in Buckhead. I went to the interview, and all six of the practice's doctors attended. At the end of the interview, Dr. Ronald Goldstein, one of the head partners of the practice, stood up and said to me, "Welcome aboard." It has been a great journey with them! The doctors and staff are amazing, kind, respectful and loving. It was a huge blessing for me and I was thrilled and blessed to be a part of such an amazing team. I could never forget this love.

A year after starting my career as a business associate at Goldstein, Garber, and Salama, I decided to apply for my

American citizenship. I took the citizenship test and passed it without any issues. Shortly afterward, I was called back for an interview and was issued my certificate of American citizenship just two weeks later. We planned a big party to celebrate my new citizenship. At the time, Josephine and I were living at the Brandon Mills condos in Dunwoody, a suburb of Atlanta. We rented the clubhouse and invited our friends and the staff and doctors from Dr. Goldstein's office. It was a hot party—so hot the tables caught on fire! We put the flames out and continued partying until two in the morning. We had a blast, and I got to be the DJ for the event. We were one big GGS family, and we all got closer and closer as time passed.

After joining Dr. Goldstein, Dr. Garber, and Dr. Salama's dental practice, not only did I learn a lot about the importance of oral care, but I was also exposed to meeting so many wonderful, genuine people who are successful and do not look down on small people.

I also had the opportunity to meet many Hollywood actors and actresses who come to our dental practice for treatment and to make their smiles better. I am amazed to see so many patients who fly in from out of state and even out of the country for their oral treatment.

Growing up in an African village, we would use chewing sticks for teeth cleaning. When I visited a dentist here in the US for the first time to have a teeth cleaning, I thought the dentist would say, "Victor, you will need dentures." Surprisingly, he did not notice any problem with my teeth. No cavities and no decay.

I remember when I went to have my wisdom teeth extracted. After the extraction, the doctor told me my teeth were so strong that they broke his instrument. Maybe the chewing sticks and zebra juice helped. (Just kidding about the zebra juice.) Now I am educating my family members about the importance of good oral care and the effects if oral care is neglected.

Joining the team at Goldstein, Garber, and Salama started the development of a lifelong partnership with the staff, patients, and doctors at the practice. Goldstein, Garber, and Salama employees are diverse—it's like the United Nations, with staff members from different nationalities; Canada, India, Brazil, Israel, Egypt, South Africa, Nigeria, Columbia, Mexico, Italy, France, Puerto Rico, Pakistan, and so on. We get along very well, like one big family. It was a big transition for me coming from a big hospital where there were more than three hundred staff members—doctors, nurses, and business personnel—to a dental practice of over forty, but there were some similarities as well.

When I started working with Drs. Goldstein, Garber, and Salama, a couple of months in, I was passing Dr. Goldstein's exam room when he asked me to get him a temp bond (this is used to bond a temporary crown). I thought he asked me to get him a tampon. When I went to Gina, who was in charge of the supply room at that time, I was so embarrassed and did not know how to ask Gina for a tampon. I stood in front of the supply room for a few minutes, then went in and told Gina Dr. Goldstein had sent me to get him a tampon. Gina asked me if I was sure, I said, "I think that's what he asked for." Gina was not convinced, so she went with me to go and ask Dr. Goldstein what he wanted. When we asked Dr. Goldstein, he told us he wanted a *temp bond*, the materials for bonding temporary crowns ... That was an LOL moment.

A few months after that event, the scheduling coordinator asked me to help her locate a chart in the attic where we store most of our patient charts. The name she sent me to search for was "Kipple," and, of course, when I was in the attic, I was searching for the last name "Nipple." After fifteen minutes of searching, I had no luck finding Nipple's chart. When I came down from the attic, she asked me if I found Kipple's chart, and I told her I had been looking for Nipple's chart. It felt like I had a one-track mind. I thought she said the word Nipple—the two words sound alike. The scheduling coordinator burst out laughing. Thank God, I wasn't kicked out or sent to an ear doctor to hear better.

The next incident happened when I walked into the break room one day. The break room was so close to my office, I heard the ladies chat when they'd eat lunch. I tried to keep to myself and not share what I heard, and sometimes I'd wait till everyone had eaten before I got to eat my lunch, so I didn't listen too much. One day, I was grabbing water from the fridge, and I couldn't help but hear the ladies talking and laughing in the break room—Gina was showing the girls her new bra. I immediately closed one of my eyes, but she didn't worry, she didn't mind because it was just me, Victor. I got my water and left the break room.

I saw and heard a lot and kept it all to myself. Again, I was happy to be a part of this lovely practice, where love, care, humility, and respect was the norm. My parents always told me to do my best even when nobody was looking. They raised me and my siblings to be independent, hard-working, honest, helpful, and respectful and I have successfully demonstrated those teachings throughout the years. In the year 2000, the doctor decided to start handing out the Employee of the Year award at the office holiday party, which was held at the Hyatt hotel in Buckhead at Christmas time. The staff and doctors would nominate the person who best deserved the award based on work ethic and character. The winner was announced at the holiday party, and to my surprise it was me. I won the award the following year as well, and the many years to follow.

The years passed and I humbly continued to win the nomination for the employee of the year—so much so, that finally, the doctors had a meeting and decided it would be ideal to give the other team members the opportunity to receive the award, which I thought was quite fair. One year, my wife was invited to the holiday party, which was a huge surprise because the celebration had always been strictly staff-only, and in addition, the president of Spelman College, Dr. Johnnetta Cole, was there as well. I thought this was odd but did not take any serious consideration as to why at the time. After everyone had eaten, Dr. Cole stood up in front of everyone and surprised us with a speech saying really nice things about me. She went on to discuss the Employee of the Year award and determined the award should be named after me. I was dumbfounded and rather shocked, to say the least! A lot of my coworkers and myself were in tears—to say I was speechless about this honor would be an understatement.

Once Dr. Cole was finished, Dr. Ronald Goldstein took the stage. He had written a summary regarding the award. His words were, "Twenty years ago, a shy young man left his village in Africa to come to America. He came to earn a degree and make his family proud of him. This week, the dental practice of Goldstein, Garber, and Salama established the Victor Award in the name of Victor Ekworomadu, formally referred to as the Employee of the Year Award. The award was established in honor of Victor Ekworomadu, the man whose influence has become almost legendary to the individuals and businesses he associates with daily." Dr. Goldstein continued by saying, "What is unique about Victor is that he has not succumbed to the Western standards he is surrounded by. He has remained true to the values he was instilled with from childhood."

He went on to say, "Victor began his employment at Goldstein,

Garber, and Salama in 1994. At first, his responsibilities were assisting the doctors, but as his skills and character became evident, he was quickly given increased responsibilities. The doctors who hired him had no idea how important his role would become in day-to-day operations. Despite his low-key approach and quiet manner, Victor stood out with his sincerity in wanting to help people and his sensitivity to people in need. As this dental practice was already known around the world for the quality of its cosmetic dentistry, Victor's contributions helped the level of care and professionalism rise. His influence was not limited to the staff he works with, but with patients coming for dental treatment beginning to ask for Victor. The suppliers and service people insisted that a visit wasn't complete without Victor's handshake. In addition to his job with Drs. Goldstein, Garber, and Salama, Victor coordinated a food and clothing ministry on behalf of his church in Marietta."

Reviewing Dr. Goldstein's comments allowed me to give credit to my parents who raised me. They did so well to instill in me a standard to live by that I still practice to this day. Even though they are no longer with us, if they were to look down from where they are, I would want them to tell me, "Well done."

Not only was I presented the employee of the year award, but I was also awarded a one-week trip to Puerto Rico, all expenses paid! That included airplane tickets, accommodations, and meals. When I was granted the trip, my manager at the time, Gail Cummings, booked the trip for us.

On the day of the trip, a limo was sent to our house to pick Josephine and me up to take us to the airport. Once we arrived in Puerto Rico, we picked up our luggage, and a young lady was waiting for us with a sign who happened to be our limo driver. She drove us from the airport to a very beautiful and private house right on the beach. As soon as we entered, we were greeted by the most beautiful flowers in the center of the table. We were even treated to a refrigerator filled with snacks and drinks. Though, I forgot my funnel (LOL)—we were like kids in a candy store!

On the next day, a golf cart was delivered to us so we could drive around the resort. Every morning, we had a buffet breakfast including eggs, waffles, fruits, juices, and so much more. Coincidentally, Dr. Goldstein and Dr. Garber were lecturing with a group of doctors who came from all around the United States, and we had an opportunity to attend some of the lectures. Around dinner time, we met with the doctors at a restaurant which had live music and an incredible dinner menu. The employees at the resort were very friendly—as a matter of fact, we befriended many of them.

We went to the beach a couple of times and one day, during our stay, we traveled to San Juan for sightseeing. We saw some people booking cruise ships and some returning from cruises. On the last day of our stay, we took a few photos with the friends we'd made. We had such a great time it was hard to say goodbye. That was one of my favorite vacations I'd ever been on.

On the day of our departure, the limo came and picked us up to take us to the airport. Once we arrived in Atlanta, the limo came to pick us up to take us home. I must have gained ten pounds during the trip!

Winning this special trip reminded me of my father's word of wisdom, "If a child washes his or her hands, he or she eats with the king."

Every year now, at the office holiday party, I have the honor of presenting the Victor Award to the employee of the year. After almost thirty years with GGS, I cannot think of a better place to work. The group and staff at Goldstein Garber & Salama have been so caring, supportive, genuine, generous, and humble toward me and everyone they encounter. I cannot reiterate enough how thankful I am to be a part of this remarkable team.

Drs. Goldstein, Garber, Salama (GGS) and Staff Reunion and Appreciation Event

I initiated and planned this event to celebrate the past and future of GGS. This event brought together many staff members who are currently working with GGS and also those who left the practice ten to twenty years ago. I also thought this would be the right time to have it because Dr. Goldstein and Dr. Garber will be retiring. The event was successful and enjoyable for all who attended.

I was making a welcome speech to all the people who came to the reunion.

Everyone was at the GGS reception area watching a PowerPoint video of the doctors and staff.

Holiday Award Dinner

The Victor Award is presented to the employee of the year at the GGS holiday award dinner, and has been going since 1999. It is an event everyone looks forward to.

African Village Man Kills Lion with a Pencil

After I made a speech about the love, respect, and care GGS has for their patients and staff, Dr. Salama gave me a hug in appreciation with Dr. Goldstein behind us.

Chapter 8: Baby Fever

With the pressure of getting married gone and finally being situated in my career, my family began pressuring me about having children and starting a family of my own. We had been married for a few years, and my mom was inquiring when she could be expecting to have a grandchild from us so she could name him. I said to myself, *God's time is the best time, not mine.*

One day, my wife was listening to a Christian radio station out of Northern Atlanta, and they had an announcement about a young lady who had a child but was unable to care for the baby. We discussed this in detail and decided to make the call to pursue the adoption process.

The process was started by registering for orientation and training with the Bethany Christian Adoption Agency. The orientation and training took weeks to finish, but upon completion, we were appointed to meet the director handling the case at this particular agency several miles northwest of Atlanta. We waited for hours but she never showed up for the appointment. She later called us and told us she was going to have to reschedule our appointment to meet the baby and the mother because she was stuck in court. When we came back for the second meeting, we met the director, but not the young mother of the child because the mother was in the hospital. We asked about everything they would need to proceed with the adoption and the director said she would mail us the paperwork we needed. We were also shown a picture of the baby boy. He was such a handsome little guy, and we were both so excited to meet him! Once we got home, we started buying everything we would need for the new baby, but unfortunately, after a week of waiting on the paperwork, we received disappointing news from the director that said the baby's father went to the hospital, causing trouble, while the mother was there and refused to allow his son to be given up for adoption. The story seemed rather fishy, and suspicions were confirmed when we discovered the director chose another family to adopt the little boy, but she didn't mention why she did not choose us. Also, the director had never mentioned money to us in order to care for the baby, we were more than willing to help the mother and the baby if the agency requested it.

With this door closing on us, another door opened in our life. We reached out to another adoption agency where we met with the director and paid a small registration fee to ensure the care of the child and to process the paperwork. After paying the fee for the registration, we attended several meetings pertaining to the adoption and they asked for $20,000, upfront, to adopt a child. We asked ourselves why they were asking for so much, they literally had a price for the baby's life.

Facing one disappointment after another, our patience was quickly running thin. One day, I was discussing the situation with my sister-in-law who lived in Texas. She was very sympathetic and told us she would reach out to her brother in Nigeria who was a medical doctor who cared for children at a children's home (an orphanage). After a couple of days, I received an email from him saying he'd seen a boy just a few months old at the home we may be interested in. We ran a series of medical physicals on him and everything checked out quite well. I quickly followed up with the phone call and inquired what the necessary protocol was to start an international adoption. He sent an email application from the orphanage to us, which we filled out and submitted to the orphanage, and to our joy, they approved our application!

Back home in Nigeria, around the same time, I had gotten the sad news my mother had passed away at the age of ninety-three. I believe she should still be alive today, but unfortunately, she suffered from complications following a glaucoma surgery and had lost her sight. In addition, her heart was broken over the losses of her oldest son, her youngest sister, and her younger brother, all very close to the same time. Shortly before she passed, I had a conversation with her to see how she was doing, and I could tell she was upset and would complain about the fact that her youngest family members, the ones who would in theory bury her when her time came, were passing before her. I was touched by this conversation with her in years to come, and appreciated her even more, for she was a strong and dedicated woman who was a passionate caregiver to me, my siblings, and other families in the village. My father passed away when I was young, so it was up to my mother to raise us. She did a great job, for all of us successfully graduated college and continued with successful careers. Her death hit me hard, but I was so grateful she raised me and my siblings as she did.

I decided to combine the trips and go to my mother's funeral as well as visit the children's home. This was very difficult to accomplish because the village where my mom's funeral was being held was very far away from the children's home. After the service was over, I flew to Lagos, rested for a few days, and flew to the Enugu airport. From there, I hired a taxi and took an eight-hour drive down the dirt road to the orphanage. By the time we were close, it was getting late and dark, so my family suggested visiting the children's home in the morning.

We went the next day and met the little boy we wanted to adopt. He was six months old at the time. I got to hold him, and he stared right back. I looked around the room and saw there was also a little girl about the same age as the boy, and considered adopting her as soon as I could finalize his adoption. Little did I know, the entire process of adopting this child would be so difficult and challenging. We met with the director briefly and she assured me there was a possibility I would be able to take the boy home with me after the funeral was over.

It was a ten-hour drive back to the village where my mom's funeral was taking place. There were about six hundred to seven hundred people who attended her service, which was very lovely and all of the guests were pleased as well. Afterward, I drove the ten hours back again to the children's home. When I got there, they informed me the adoption paperwork had not been finished, so he was not ready to leave. So again, I traveled the eight hours back to the Enugu airport, then flew to Lagos, then Amsterdam, and then the US, without our child. Between planning and attending my mother's funeral and the problems that came up regarding the adoption, it was one of the most difficult trips in my life.

I returned to the States after the funeral with a heavy heart and a lot to think about. I could not stop thinking about my mother and her legacy, as well as the child waiting for us back in Nigeria. At my mother's service, the bishop read the eulogy and said some things that hit me like a brick to the face. He discussed the impact my mother had on the community and the women and children she provided aid to. These were amazing and inspirational things to be remembered for.

"When you leave this world behind, people are not going to remember what kind of car you drove or how big your house was, but how you treated people and the impact you had in their lives." The bishop's words pushed my wife and me to put together a ministry to help the homeless and less fortunate, called Hope and Love for Families of Georgia Inc. Forming our Hope and Love charity distracted us from the stresses and setbacks of our hopeful adoption.

The nonprofit organization was established in 2003, not only to give our wandering and worried minds something positive to focus on, but to continue with the legacy my mother left behind. The primary mission of Hope and Love charity was to provide assistance to struggling families and organizations. Many of these families tend to fall under the radar and are often not eligible for government assistance, so individuals and families are given funds to assist with temporary living arrangements, utility payments, as well as food and clothing. We have helped families dealing with domestic abuse by providing hotel payments and food, and over the years, we have helped several notable organizations and shelters in the Atlanta area including MUST Ministries, the Atlanta Mission, Seven Bridges to Recovery, the Wounded Warriors Project, and the Cobb County Senior Center. Hope and Love has been able to assist the shelters and organizations with much-needed clothing, linens, toiletries, gift cards, donations, and cleaning supplies. In addition to supplies, we have put together meals and goodie bags, and serve sandwiches and coffee alongside these notable organizations through the streets of Atlanta, where we meet those most in need, face-to-face. We have also been able to bless several schools with much-needed supplies for both teachers and students. The organization works closely with several groups of teenagers in metro Atlanta school systems by providing them with a way to give back to their communities. These youngsters volunteer time with the organization, helping put together charity yard sales and assembling gift bags for the homeless, in exchange for school community service time. Hope and Love has assisted over eight hundred needy families in the Atlanta area since its start in 2003. Hope and Love charity has not received any government grants, but relies solely on private donations from individual donors and charity yard sales. The organization may be small, but we have a big heart.

I have served in food ministries as well as been a deacon and usher at the church for years. This influence has greatly helped me to recognize the words of God and put them to use. There are six full-time board members responsible for the decision-making, and they are all passionate about serving the community and helping the less fortunate. All board members have full-time jobs outside of the organization and do not receive any payment from Hope and Love. Our board members organize meetings, collections, drop-offs, and direct food and clothing drives.

Hope and Love charity was proving successful and made a huge impact on the community, but we were still waiting for word on our child. We continued to intensify our adoption efforts and my sister-in-law's family back in Nigeria was helping supply all the necessary documentation to complete the process. After a couple of weeks, we received an email from the children's home that said the state government enacted a decree that no adopted child could leave the country—that way, the state government had better access to the newly adopted child and could easily monitor. This was just more frustrating news and yet another setback. At this point, we felt the situation was in God's hands and all we could do was wait and pray. We went back to focusing on growing our ministries in the meantime.

On March 23, 2003, we received an email from my in-laws in Africa saying they had agreed to proceed with the adoption. This was all thanks to the influence and persistence my in-laws had over the children's home. Because they were so actively involved with the children's home itself, they did not see it fair to deny the adoption request. At this point, they had asked us to name the baby, and we named him Ezra. We submitted all the necessary documents to the United States immigration office in Atlanta, and after a couple of weeks, we received a certification of adoption—though they misspelled Ezra to say Ezera. While this child was waiting for us to get him, we kept sending document after document between the immigration office and the children's home. The immigration office claimed they never received the documents or the certificate we had mailed to them. After we were sent all the necessary documents, months went by and we did not hear from them. My wife decided to call and check the status of the adoption and she was told just to wait and be patient. After several more months, we received another notice from immigration saying the social workers who did the home study were not in the adoption report. We immediately called the social worker and asked for the report to be revised and to include the license number and expiration date, which were supposedly missing from the original report. After a few days, we received yet another letter from the immigration saying the home study report did not include our financial report. We called the social worker back and asked her to revise the home study report again.

We personally looked through the original requirements again and saw that none of the changes were made. We thought we had given them everything they needed. A couple of days later, we received another letter asking us to provide proof of payment regarding a traffic ticket my wife had paid for back when she lived in New Jersey in 1990. One day, instead of an email, I called my in-law in Nigeria. He said there were families at the children's home trying to pay a lot of money to take the boy away. He appealed to them to release our son, and our appeal was granted, so we had to go to court so the judge could come to an agreement. My in-laws represented and defended us on our behalf in the court and won! I called my brother in Nigeria and he flew my niece Chichi into the children's home so she could bring our son to Lagos. My niece picked up Ezra from the home and she informed me the child was skinny and dressed in dirty and torn clothes. Evidently, the money and clothing I left for him were not used to take care of him. By this time, he was one year and eight months old. It had taken nearly a year and a half just to get him out of the children's home. When he was brought to my brother's house in Lagos, my family said Ezra could not even stand on his own two legs because they were just not strong enough. They had to tie boards to his legs and create a makeshift brace just so he could stand and walk on his own. Of course, he was taken to the doctors for a full medical evaluation and he received treatment immediately.

My wife and I were being asked every day back in the States by our friends how the adoption process was going for us and sometimes we just did not have an answer. Since we were not sure how much longer this process was going to take, we sent the child pictures and clothes and called him nearly every day. Our phone bill was about the price of a decent mortgage after just a month. As you can imagine, the emotional drain and uncertainty were taking a hefty toll on us. Our Ezra was waiting for us thousands of miles away, and yet we still had not heard a word from immigration. After a while, we contacted Senator Johnny Isakson to help us, and like everyone else, he told us we just had to wait a while longer. We contacted another government official, a congresswoman, Denise Majette, from another district, to intervene. Although she was not in our district, she knew all the right people to contact to help us. She was persistent with these other officials and insisted that if they did not help us, she would cross over to the district to handle the situation herself.

Eventually, we did get a letter from the immigration office requesting more documents, some of which had already been submitted. They also requested to get Ezra's fingerprints, which we sent over to the director of the children's home along with additional documentation. After a couple of days, we received a letter from the children's home stating the Department of US Immigration had sent us a form to fill in to complete on the welfare of the baby. They also stated they needed to see him and personally check his welfare before releasing the baby from the family in Lagos. So, they sent a representative who would fly in and observe my family with Ezra. I made sure to send enough funds to my brother to cover all the expenses for the representative staying with them. The representative and my brother signed the forms and sent them to US immigration, which contacted us within two weeks. We received yet another letter from immigration telling us the home study was not properly revised. Apparently the agents failed to include a clearance letter from children's welfare services saying that Ezra was not involved in abuse. Of course, when we tried to reach out to the agent, she was out of the country so we would have to wait for her to come back to do the revisions.

I considered hiring an attorney, thinking maybe it would help speed up the process. It wasn't any help and the attorney fee was a waste of money. At this point, we did not know what else we should do. I contacted the government offices again and they contacted the immigration office. Within a few days, we received a letter of approval with no explanation as to what we needed to do next. When we called the number on the letter to see what the next step was, they told us they had done their part and that our next step was to call the visa office in New Hampshire for further information. The visa office informed us a file had been sent to the US Consulate in Lagos, which would notify us of an interview date.

Every day, I got up at two a.m. to call the embassy in Nigeria to check if they received our documents and if they knew of our interview date. Sometimes, the phone would ring for minutes with no answer. Other times, it would just stay busy or the call would drop, making it impossible to reach anyone. We dealt with this for a couple of weeks until, one day, I was able to get a hold of someone in the embassy. I gave her the file number, but she said she did not have any information about the case. The conversation with her was going nowhere fast, so I hung up. We sent an email to the embassy with the file number and case information, but there was no response there either. After a couple of weeks of not receiving a response, I tried calling again.

Finally, four weeks after we initially sent the file to the embassy and were unable to reach anyone, the phone rang and someone picked up on the second ring. I gave him the file and the case information and he told me they just received the file. He asked me when we could go in for an interview and where we would like our package sent, so I immediately gave him my brother's address in Lagos. It was two thirty in the morning and I was running around like a chicken with my head cut off, trying to find a calendar so we could plan and schedule an interview. We expected to stay overseas for about two weeks, which we thought was sufficient time to obtain a visa for Ezra and fly back to the States.

The flight we scheduled would land on May 1, 2004, and we planned the interview for the third. We received about fifty pages of documents the day leading up to our departure to get our son — these forms included fingerprints, police records, medical reports, and so much more. I quickly forwarded everything to my brother, who was caring for Ezra. Leaving no stone unturned, we contacted the immigration office in Atlanta to ask them if there was anything else we would need before our interview. They told us to go to the US consulate in Lagos and ask them, so of course we called several times before we got a response. We asked them if there was anything else we needed, and they said to just be prepared for the interview. To verify this, I called again and spoke to another representative, but received the same answer.

With our trip and the interview quickly approaching, we finalized the booking for the flights and did some shopping for our Nigerian family. On Wednesday, three days before we were scheduled to fly out, we received a letter from immigration stating we needed to redo the fingerprints or else we could not move forward with the interview. Usually, fingerprints were done by appointment only. When we called to schedule an appointment, we were told they were booked solid through the next couple of weeks. We were absolutely dumbfounded.

I mentioned it to one of my coworkers, and coincidentally, she had an appointment scheduled with a secretary of a US government official. She immediately called him and told him about our situation, who then made a prompt call to the immigration office. This was Thursday, two days before we were scheduled to fly out. He advised us to purchase a money order and go downtown to the immigration office in Atlanta to obtain a letter of approval for fingerprints. At this point, it was almost one p.m. and the office closed at three. We immediately rushed downtown to the immigration office, picked up the fingerprint document, and rushed back to Buford Highway (several miles away in Atlanta traffic) for the appointment itself. They saw us immediately and shut the door behind us. There were several people ahead of us in line, but we waited and eventually got through. We finally had our fingerprints done and they were promptly forwarded to the US embassy in Lagos—this alone usually takes a week to get the report back. We were emotionally and physically worn out from all of the constant back and forth. We just wanted this to be over and be home with our new family.

That Saturday, I went to the store to pick up a few things for the trip and for my family. While I was out, my wife called me in a panic to tell me that KLM Airlines had called to tell us our flight reservations had been canceled. I was in shock, and could not believe what I was hearing. I dropped everything I was doing, went home, and immediately called the airline. Apparently, I had made two reservations, but they canceled one. We were able to fix everything and finish packing and gathered hundreds of pages of documents in the few hours ahead of our departure.

The flight took off at six p.m. Atlanta time and we landed at eight thirty p.m. Nigerian time the next day. By the time we made it through customs and immigration and made it home to my brother's house, it was nearly ten p.m. The last time I physically got to see my son was when he was six months old and he had not seen my wife at all, apart from pictures and videos. The look on his face was, "What took you so long?" Our son was almost two years old by this time, and he called my wife Auntie Mommy. We spent the next day or so resting and finalizing the never-ending pile of documents.

Tuesday was the big day! We got up early at four a.m., had breakfast, and made our way over to the US embassy. We got there at six a.m., even though our appointment was scheduled for seven thirty, and patiently waited in line until the embassy opened. Upon entering, the security guards told us only one parent could go in. I prayed to God to give me strength, energy, and patience, for our boy was very active and hard to contain, plus I was walking around with a hundred or so documents, and I was roasting inside my suit—sweating like a firefighter and my shirt and suit were soaked. The security guard saw me and noticed I needed a hand controlling Ezra. He immediately went outside and found my wife and asked her to come in and help contain his endless energy. We were there for hours, despite having an appointment, but nobody called us and at two forty-five, we approached the window and asked the clerk what time they closed and that we had an appointment scheduled for seven thirty that morning but nobody had called us. She told us to go home and come back the next morning.

Disappointed and frustrated, we did as we were told and returned bright and early the next day. We waited several more hours before they finally called us in. They were drilling me with ridiculous questions, like the correct spelling of our son's name, how long I'd lived in the US, and when my last visit to Nigeria was. I answered all the questions honestly and to the best of my knowledge. After we were finished, the clerk sent us home and told us to come back again the next day at one thirty because they still needed to verify a few things. This prompted me to contact the airlines and change my return flight, which I had to pay an extra fine for.

The following morning, my brother went to work and instructed his wife to take us to the embassy. When we were about to leave, she could not find her car keys—we all looked everywhere but still could not find them. The embassy was very far away from my brother's house, and with traffic, it could take up to two hours to get there. Thank God my brother had a couple of extra vehicles, an older car he had not driven for at least six months, and another car that *conveniently* had the keys locked in the ignition. I was dumbfounded. Here we were, in a hurry to get to the embassy, and we had one car that needed work, another with missing keys, and another with the keys locked in it. We immediately called for a mechanic to come help us. On a hunch, I had the mechanic check the third vehicle that had not been driven in several months, and to our luck, it just needed a new battery and a couple of other quick fixes. I had the mechanic address those issues and, soon enough, we were on our way again. The traffic was terrible on the way to the embassy with so many accidents. Thank God, we arrived on time despite the countless setbacks that morning.

We waited at the embassy for hours, but no one called our name. At around two fifty, we approached the window again and asked the clerk if we would be able to get the visa we needed that day. She asked us to wait a few minutes while she went to the back and verified a few things. The clerk informed us the officer handling the case had already left for the day and that we should come back tomorrow. Tears of frustration filled my eyes. Despite Ezra being so young and not knowing what was going on, he sat very quietly and calmly and waited. Again, we went home, changed our flights, and prepared to return to the embassy the very next day.

And the next day was like a dream come true!

We got there and they finally issued us a visa for our son. Joy, relief, and happiness came into the room. My family had been patiently waiting outside, and the joy was evident in their shouts as we exited the embassy. They were jumping and rejoicing for us. We all went back to my brother's house, had dinner, and celebrated this achievement. We finished the adoption process, got Ezra's visa, and we were ready to take our son home to start the next chapter of our lives.

Throughout all the joy, we saw sadness in the eyes of my brother and his wife. My brother had pretty much raised Ezra and the three of them grew quite attached to each other. It was going to be hard to separate them.

On the day we were scheduled to fly home, my brother and sister-in-law drove us to the airport. My brother managed to escort us through the terminal while my sister-in-law could not stop the tears from flowing. It was difficult to say goodbye to the child they had taken such amazing care of for the past year and several months. Our flight took off that night as planned, with a brief layover in Amsterdam. While we were there going through immigration, an officer was asking us for a particular document the US embassy was supposed to give to us, but had failed to pass to us. Thankfully, we were able to work things out and he eventually let us board our connecting flight.

We landed in Atlanta hours later, ending this trying journey. My coworker was already there, waiting to pick us up from the airport and take us home. Another coworker, Gail Heyman, called to check on us and ask if she could be Ezra's grandma. We all agreed and said it would be an honor to have her as part of the family. She arranged for his first school, which was a Jewish school, and Gail gave Ezra so much love and participated in every grandparent event in Ezra's school and the activities involved in his life. He seemed to enjoy the school and quickly made several friends, and stayed at that school for a couple of years until it was time to register him in kindergarten classes at a public school. He did not adjust well to changing schools. Despite being strong-willed and inquisitive, he would come home every day with negative reports from his teachers. It was always "Ezra sneezed," "Ezra laughed," "Ezra touched one of the other kids," "Ezra would not lay down for a nap," and it just kept going. It was like a broken record, and we were tired of hearing this every day.

We took him to another private school, but he was still having trouble there, likely because it was a larger class size. He was full of energy and constantly needed a lot of one-on-one attention. This was frustrating, but we understood he was going to need to be in a special school, where he could properly grow. One day, my wife was discussing school with a client at her job and the lady recommended a private school in Alpharetta called Mill Springs Academy. We were living in Marietta at the time, which was not super close to Alpharetta, but decided to give them a call to get more information. I found it interesting that the school's motto was "Teach the way children want to learn, not the way we want to teach." That really struck a good chord with us. Upon further investigation, we found there were school bus stops all over the city, which would make the commute a little easier for us. We called the headmaster and made an appointment to see him and take a tour of the school. After meeting him and the administrators, we were impressed and thrilled when he was accepted into the first grade. There were only three other children in his class, so he got the one-on-one attention he needed and he excelled at that school and even wrote a poem that was published in the school library. We found he really enjoyed reading and was reading up to three or four books a week.

Our new life together as a family was just getting started, and we could not have been happier. We began the process of planning a grand celebration to get together with all our close friends and family who so graciously prayed for and supported us over the years. We were so grateful for the encouragement we got from each person. Nearly one hundred guests came to the celebration, and it was a beautiful and happy day.

The years passed and Ezra continued attending the private school a while longer which gave him a good foundation. He began middle school and again excelled. He was in middle school and competed in the spelling geography bee. He was among the top ten out of one hundred students.

Ezra is doing well today, enrolled in Georgia State, studying graphic design. We are proud he is in college, and we know he will be successful in his future, because of the parenting and foundation we gave him.

I will not forget to thank Dr. Ronald Goldstein and Judy Goldstein, Dr. David Garber and Barbra Garber, Gail Heyman and Lyon Heyman, Candace Paetzhold and Dr. Jeff Paetzhold, and Dr. Maurice Salama and family for the love they gave Ezra. A special thank you to Ezekiel Ekworomadu and Martina Ekworomadu, and Mr. Bobby Ezor and Elisa Ezor for their help with Ezra's future. As the African adage says, "It takes a village to raise a child."

As a family, we have learned so many lessons from this journey, especially "don't give up," particularly if you have invested so much of your heart into whatever it is you are trying to accomplish. Nothing in life is easy, so you must remain persistent and determined in order to achieve your goal, and by doing so, even you could kill a lion with a pencil.

We want to acknowledge and thank all of our friends and family who have supported us through the years and helped make our dream come true. Thank you from the bottom of our hearts.

In an effort to continue the legacy of my parents, who are both sadly deceased, the next section of the story will contain my father's words of wisdom, the wisdom of the village elders, and its interpretations. His words have helped me throughout my daily life, and I hope they will have the same effect on you. I pray for good health and peace for you all.

When Ezra First Arrived, 2005

Ezra was three years old when the adoption was finally completed and we brought him home. My sister made a special welcome outfit for us, called a Dachiki, which we wore for the celebration. More than one hundred people attended the celebration, including former congress lady Denise Majette.

African Village Man Kills Lion with a Pencil

Ezra was six months old at the children's home

I was on my way to my mother's funeral, and I stopped by the children's home for the first time. On the right is a little girl being held by one of the ladies who worked at the home. At that time, I was thinking of adopting the little girl also, but I never thought Ezra's process would be that challenging and take that long! By the time that Ezra's adoption process was complete, I had lost all of my hair from the stress.

Ezra at age 21

Hope and Love Foundation Board Members and Events

Starting on the left, Josephine Ekworomadu, Kathleen Bufford, Victor Ekworomadu, Candace Paetzhold, and Kim Nimons. These people gave their time and energy while holding full-time jobs and raising their families. Hope and Love participates in several events, ranging from fundraising yard sales, nonperishable food drives, and distributing food to the homeless on the streets and in shelters in the community.

African Village Man Kills Lion with a Pencil

Josephine's cousin and I were loading supplies to be distributed to the homeless shelters in the city.

Gallery

The top picture is Dr. Goldstein and the bottom picture is Dr. David Garber making speeches at the Ekworomadu family reunion.

Employee of the year winner award trip to Puerto Rico.

African Village Man Kills Lion with a Pencil

Bowling Office Event

Goldstein Garber & Salama team event. This event took place at the main event. We all had lots of fun and built relationships outside of the office. Other team bonding events we've had in the past include going to the Braves stadium and Top Gold. At Top Golf, I played so well I felt ready to challenge a champion!

Victor Ekworomadu

The Village Market

The village I grew up in is called Eke-Oba. The church we all attended is called Methodist Church Eke-Oba, and everyone collected their mail at the church every Sunday, after service.

Eke-Oba also operates a market every eighth day of the month which is called Eke Market Day. People bring their products to be sold. That is also where my mom sold her yams, corn, palm oil, peanuts, etc.

Methodist was the church we attended.

Dr. Oliver Amugo

From left to right is my niece Peace Eze , Charles Amugo (who is resting in peace), Justina (Dr. Oliver's sister), my senior brother Nathaniel Ekworomadu (who is also resting peacefully), Dr. Oliver Amugo, my brother Samuel Ekworomadu, my other brother Ezekiel Ekworomadu and a family friend.

Dr. Oliver Amugo is my brother-in-law, and the person who introduced us to Ezra. He goes to the orphanage to treat the children and offers financial assistance when needed. This picture is a celebration when he finished medical school in Nigeria. He graduated from the University of Nigeria. He now has his own practice in Abuja.

African Village Man Kills Lion with a Pencil

Hope and Love Events

We made sandwiches and loaded various supplies to be distributed to the homeless under the bridges in Metro Atlanta. Our group of volunteers also participated during Christmas to distribute nonperishable canned foods, blankets, coats, toiletries, etc. to the less fortunate families.

Victor Ekworomadu

Ezra serving coffee and pastries to the homeless in the street in downtown Atlanta.

African Village Man Kills Lion with a Pencil

Certificates

I received certificates of honors every year throughout my college days. Other certificates included the certificate of appreciation from Kennestone Hospital Volunteer System, outstanding employee recognition from Dr. Goldstein, performance recognition certificate from North Fulton Hospital, Gold award from Drs. Goldstein, Garber, and Salama, and employee of the year award from Drs. Goldstein, Garber, and Salama, a certificate of appreciation from Mountains of Praise church in appreciation of community service, and a plaque of appreciation from North Ridge Country Club Texas.

Victor Ekworomadu

AUXILIARY
SHALLOWFORD HOSPITAL

"CONCERNED ABOUT YOU"

March 29, 1993

RE: Victor Ekworomadu

Victor Ekworomadu joined the volunteers of Shallowford Hospital Auxiliary in 1990. He was placed in Radiology where he showed intense interest.

He has been loyal to his volunteer commitment, going beyond the call of duty, despite holding down a full time job. He is a fine gentleman who is honest, kind, thoughtful and hard working.

Yours very truly,

Bev Warner
Past President
Shallowford Hospital
Auxiliary
Phone 396-6722

 4575 NORTH SHALLOWFORD RD. • DUNWOODY, GEORGIA 30338 • (404) 454-2000
A MEMBER OF THE CHARTER MEDICAL CORPORATION FAMILY OF QUALITY HEALTH CARE FACILITIES.

Certificate of Merit 1982

Certificate of Merit 1983

Philander Smith College
Little Rock, Arkansas

Certificate of Award and Merit

Alpha Kappa Mu Honor Society

Pi Sigma Kappa Chapter

This is to certify that this Honor Certificate is being awarded **Victor C. Ekworomadu** in recognition of outstanding Scholarship Achievement during **Spring** Semester 19 **84**

Awarded this **22nd** day of **October** 19 **84**

Certificate of Merit 1984

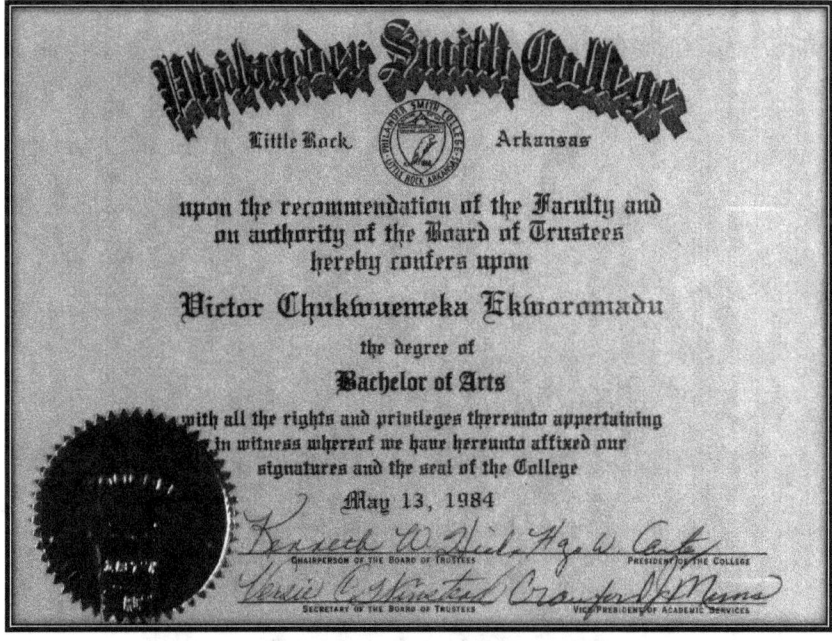

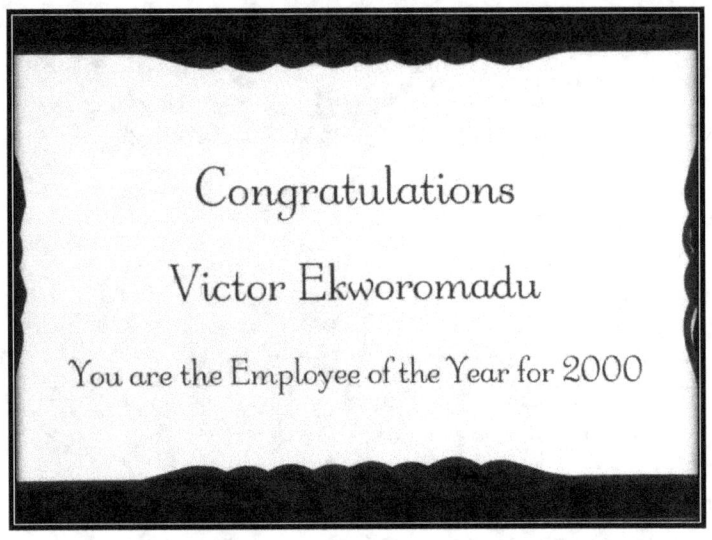

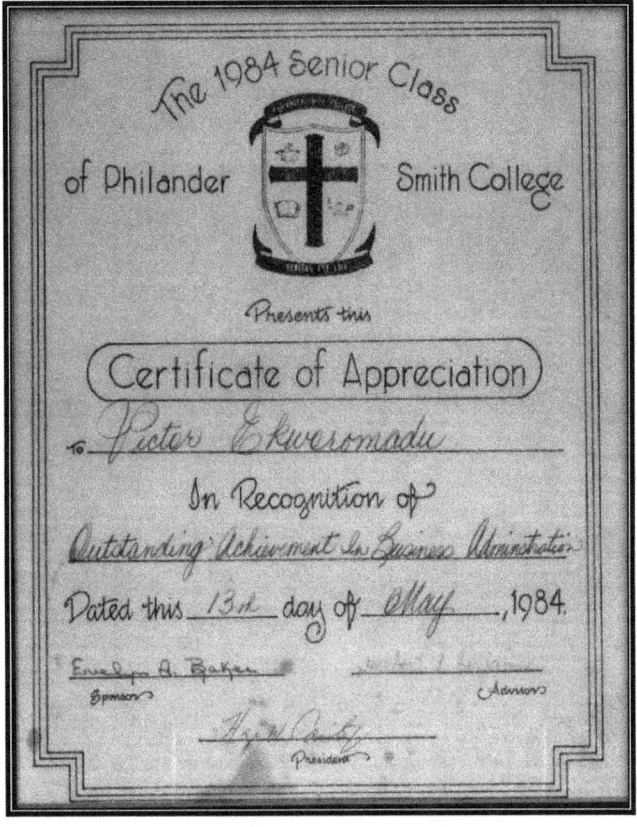

The Victor Award
Prestigious Atlanta Dental Practice Establishes New Honor

ATLANTA — Twenty years ago, a shy young man came from his village in Nigeria to America. He came to earn a degree and "make his family proud" of him. This week the dental practice of Goldstein, Garber, Salama & Gribble established the Victor Award in the name of Victor Ekworomadu.

Formerly referred to as the Employee of the Year Award, the Victor Award was established to honor Victor Ekworomadu, the man whose influence has become almost legendary to the individuals and businesses he associates with daily. In a surprise ceremony, Dr. Johnnetta Cole was pleased to make the announcement to establish the award honoring the unique qualities of this staff member, who has raised the standard of service in this Atlanta dental practice.

According to Dr. Ronald Goldstein, "What's unique about Victor is that he has not succumbed to the western standards he is surrounded with here. He has remained true to the values that he was instilled with from childhood."

Victor's response to the announcement that the award would bear his name was, "It makes me happy for my family. They would be pleased to know I have gotten this recognition."

Victor began his career at Goldstein, Garber, Salama & Gribble in 1994. At first, his responsibilities were assisting the doctors, but as his skills and character became evident, he was quickly given increased responsibilities. The doctors who hired him had no idea how positive and important his role would become in day-to-day operations. In spite of his low-key approach and quiet manner, Victor stood out with his sincerity in wanting to help people and sensitivity to others' needs. As the practice was already known around the world for the quality of their cosmetic dentistry, Victor's contributions helped the level of care and professionalism rise. His influence was not limited to the staff he works with, but patients coming for dental treatment began to ask for Victor. Then the suppliers and service people insisted that a visit wasn't complete without Victor's handshake.

In addition to his job at Goldstein, Garber, Salama & Gribble, Victor coordinates a food and clothing ministry each Sunday on behalf of his church in Marietta.

#

PHOTO Caption: Participating in the Victor Award presentation (l-r) Dr. David Garber, Victor Ekworomadu, Dr. Johnnetta Cole, Dr. Ronald Goldstein at the Grand Hyatt Hotel, December 16.

Dr. Johnette Betsch Cole presented the Victor Award at the Hyatt Hotel in Buckhead at the Goldstein Garber & Salama holiday luncheon.

African Village Man Kills Lion with a Pencil

Victor Ekworomadu

PROFESSIONAL STERILE SYSTEMS, INC
WILLIAM OAKES

351 PIKE BLVD #140 – LAWRENCEVILLE, GEORGIA 30246 – USA
Phone 770-962-2425 ~ Fax 770-962-2391

March 07, 1997

Doctor Ronald Goldstein
West Paces Profesional Park, Suite 2
1218 West Paces Ferry Rd. NE
Atlanta, Georgia 30327

Dear Doctor Goldstein,

I am writing to you to thank you for the business that you are kind enough to allow me to conduct with yourself and your staff. I am always treated well by Regina and by all of the members of your staff. It is indeed my priveledge to be able to work with you all and I thank you.

I wanted to take this opportunity to say just how impressed I am with one of your staff members. This person is without a doubt one of the most courteous, genuine, and kindhearted individuals that I have ever met. I am referring to Victor.

Without fail, when I enter your practice, Victor is there with a smiling face and a kind word. Part of my service to you folks is that I personally deliver your orders to you. So in reality, I am just one of the countless people who enter your practice in a delivery capacity. In spite of this Victor always makes me feel both valued and welcome.

This man is a true gentleman and what every employer hopes for in an employee. The world would certainly be a better place if it only had more people in it like Victor.

I just thought that you might like to know what a good impression Victor makes on the people who enter your practice.

Again, thank you for your continued support of myself and my company. I appreciate you and your staff!

Sincerely,

Bill

William Oakes

PART II

Wisdom from the Nigerian Elders

The word "wisdom" has many definitions. The definition that comes to mind is the practical ability to make consistently good decisions in our daily lives. It can also be a viewpoint for common advice.

Words of wisdom and proverbs go hand in hand. They are generally used in many African countries like Nigeria. They are used to express general truth, to teach, to reinforce morals, and to mediate disputes so individuals are not intimidated. Words of wisdom and proverbs aid in understanding and inspire people to make the right decisions. They are also used to impart knowledge and offer advice to people.

My father's name was Ekworomadu Ogbonna. He grew up in a village in Africa during a time of British rule and colonization. He was a simple man, very kind, humble, and respectful, and he believed in the pillars of honesty and integrity, on which he grounded himself to for most of his life. During his life, he was highly respected within the village and served as a guide and mentor, he also taught me how to approach life, which I do even to this day.

He believed in progress and living a clean life. He was a family man who loved the people associated with him, from his immediate family to the people within the community. I can go on for days about all the good qualities he had.

He passed away when I was in high school.

Some of his favorite sayings were notable, "Whatever you're doing, always keep your hands clean," calling for the person to be honest and transparent in everything they do. Another of his quotes was, "Whatever you want to eat tomorrow, give me mine today because tomorrow is not promised."

Growing up as a child, I observed and learned a lot from him. I also watched people come to see him to resolve various disputes about loans or land. He would always speak and begin with words of wisdom (proverbs) and address their issues. Most of the time, after speaking a few words, the two parties would come to an agreement and resolve their issues through dialogue. This was essential since there was no court system in place.

These words resolved most of the issues, and his calm demeanor and approach to situations highlighted his willingness to help the community. Although my father is no longer with us today, the wisdom he imparted on me still remains and defines and shapes me into who I am. His greater impact will live on with me as long as I live.

Thinking back, I was able to remember some of the words he wanted to share, and have included them here with my own interpretations. I hope all of these may benefit you—you might have a different interpretation based on your perception.

●●●●●●●
WISDOM STORIES

There was a man in Africa, whose job it was to climb the palm and palm wine tree. He became very successful, which led to jealousy from his neighbors. One day, one of his neighbors told him he would fall. The man did not take the comment for granted. He went home and immediately cut the ropes he used to climb the tree, but he did not stop there—he also leveled the steps in his house, laid his mat on the floor, and laid down. Then he asked himself, *How am I going to fall if I do not climb?*

Interpretation of Wisdom Story: Don't fall into trouble if you know it won't benefit you.

One day, a baby lion and a baby goat met and went to the

playground to play all day. After they both went home at night, the baby lion told his mom how he played with the baby goat. The mom told him the goat was supposed to be their meal and that he should invite the goat to another playdate to eat him for lunch. On the other hand, the baby goat told his mom about the playdate he had with the baby lion, and his mom warned him about the dangers of playing with the baby lion. The next morning, the baby lion called the baby goat for another playdate.

The baby goat responded to the baby lion saying, "Whatever your mom told you, my mom told me the same thing. I'm not coming out."

Interpretation of Wisdom Story: This leads us to the saying, "Obedience is better than sacrifice."

A couple had a little baby, and though they both worked, they had a nanny to take care of the baby. One day, the nanny fed and then bathed the baby, and placed him in the crib on the patio. As the nanny went inside to do laundry, a chimpanzee came in through the unlocked gate. The chimpanzee lifted up the baby and said, "Baby, if your mother is not tricky and your father is not tricky, we will be friends forever." The nanny heard the noise and came running out. The chimpanzee laid the baby back in the crib and ran away. When the couple came back, the nanny told them what happened. The man told his wife he would not be going to work the next day, that he would load his gun and wait in case the chimpanzee came back. The next day, the chimpanzee came back and did the same thing. As he lifted the baby up, the man pulled the trigger. The chimpanzee carefully laid the baby down and ran out. As he was running, he said the baby's dad was tricky, and because of that, their friendship ended.

The wisdom derived from the story is that in friendships or partnerships in business, be honest, open, and not tricky, which can ruin the friendship.

Interpretation of Wisdom Story: Mistrust or deception usually ruins relationships—personal or in business—forever.

A turtle committed a crime in the animal kingdom. During a meeting, they decided to not kill the turtle but to throw him into a dumpster for seven days. On the sixth day, he started to shout to get him out, the garbage was stinky and he couldn't handle it anymore. They asked him, "For all the days you were there, wasn't the garage stinky?"

Interpretation of Wisdom Story: When people are comfortable where they are and not adaptable to change, and you go to help them better their lives, sometimes they question, "What took you so long?" "Where have you been all this time?"

In Africa, a man named himself Mr. Know All and Know Front and Back. So, one day, he went to the public restroom and didn't realize toilet paper was sticking out of his pants once he finished. When people saw it, they started laughing at him. He was walking around, bragging about how he knew everything, front and back. At this point, someone called attention to the tissue

African Village Man Kills Lion with a Pencil

sticking out of his pants and said, "Since you are Mr. Know All, Know Front and Back, did you know tissue was sticking out of your pants?"

Immediately, he acknowledged he did not know *everything*. No one knows everything but God.

Interpretation of Wisdom Story: When someone thinks he or she knows everything and does not listen to corrections or instructions, even if someone is helping them, they look small.

• • • • • • •

WISDOM WORDS WITH INTERPRETATION

If a child washes their hands, they eat with a king.

Meaning: There is a reward for good deeds, either on earth or in heaven.

If you are picking and throwing a rock with a fool, people will think, you are also a fool.

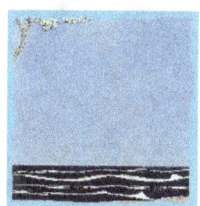

Meaning: Association brings assimilation.

You have to look at a child's face before accepting the food or candy he or she has.

Meaning: Before accepting favors from someone, make sure the favor is genuine.

He or she is a night snake, you do not know where the head is.

Meaning: Someone who is mediocre and changes opinions may be inconsistent.

In the court of law, if you judge right, right will be in your home; if you judge wrong, wrong will be in your home.

Meaning: Whatever you sow in this life, you will reap.

We learn the right road to travel by going to the wrong road.

Meaning: We learn from our mistakes.

Victor Ekworomadu

Don't be shy and swallow a hook.

Meaning: Don't be forced into doing what isn't right, under any circumstances.

Always hang your coat according to height.

Meaning: Don't buy something you can't afford to pay.

A chicken won't forget who dried his feathers when he was wet.

Meaning: Don't forget someone when they were there for you.

If you want to be a boxer, first box a bag of sand.

Meaning: If you want to have a big dream, start with a small dream and a plan.

If you fart and it doesn't smell, you will not eat a rotten egg.

Meaning: If you try your best and you have no accomplishments, don't beat yourself up over it.

African Village Man Kills Lion with a Pencil

It is easy to shoot a fly. If you shoot it, would you pick it up?

Meaning: Sometimes it is easy to start a project, just be willing to finish it.

You cannot be in a river and allow soap to enter your eyes without washing it off.

Meaning: You cannot be in the midst of prosperity and act like someone who is poor.

Whatever you want to throw away and later pick up, don't throw it too far.

Meaning: You don't burn bridges if you know you will need the person later on.

Don't bite the finger that feeds you.

Meaning: Don't be ugly to or hurt someone who is always there for you.

Victor Ekworomadu

A bird said he is going to poop in the sky. As he poops, the poop lands on his back.

Meaning: When you try to wish someone bad or evil, it will backfire and come back to haunt you.

Smiling does not mean the person is sweet or nice.

Meaning: Don't be deceived by outward looks or appearance.

If a child is crying and pointing a finger, if the child's mother is not there, the father is there.

Meaning: Sometimes things happen for a reason.

A suspect is not supposed to wear a mask.

Meaning: Don't look suspicious if you have been accused of something.

Anyone who is related to a lawyer, and a relative commits a minor crime and goes to jail, people will assume the law he practiced is irrelevant.

Meaning: If you are not competent in the training and education you received, it will be perceived that the training and education is a failure.

Someone who is eating and does not offer food to his or her children, then to someone else's children that are there, what are they waiting for?

Meaning: If you cannot help yourself in any situation, how would you be able to help someone else?

When you cut down tree branches, the leaves will not die immediately.

Meaning: Whatever you do in life, good or bad, you will pay later.

A chicken is not supposed to be shy on her eggs.

Meaning: You are not supposed to be a stranger in your own home.

Look for a black goat in the daytime while it is bright, when the night comes it will be difficult.

Meaning: Set a goal and start planning your life while you are young. If you wait and get old, it might be too late.

If you visit a frog and expect him to give you a chair, did you see him sitting on any chair?

Meaning: If you are asking a poor person for food or money, how do you expect them to have something to offer?

The woodpecker bird was saying how he would cry for weeks if his mother passes away. Unfortunately for him, when his mother passes away, he had a big cyst on his beak and was unable to cry.

Meaning: When you plan and hope your plan will go well, sometimes it fails due to no fault of your own.

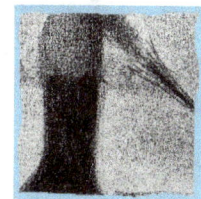

There is nothing an eye will see that will make it shed blood but tears.

Meaning: There is nothing we can hear or see that will surprise us in this generation.

You cannot outrun your Botox.

Meaning: Whatever you do in this life, good or bad, your conscience will always be with you.

If a bug kills a dog, that bug will definitely die with the dog.

Meaning: An evil person that dies will be buried with his or her evil.

If a lizard fell from the roof and nodded its head up and down and said if nobody praises him, then he will praise himself.

Meaning: If you accomplish something in your lifetime and nobody notices or recognizes it, you can pat your shoulder and celebrate your own accomplishments.

Victor Ekworomadu

If a teenager tries to lift his dad above his shoulder, the Dashiki (or wrapper the dad is wearing) will blindfold the teenager.

Meaning: If the teenager tries to outdo his or her dad but falls short or cannot cope, he or she will be humiliated.

It is not good to break a fight if you do not have a strong neck.

Meaning: It is proper to stay in your lane if you do not have what it takes.

It is not proper for the guest you invited to your house to share the meat in your soup.

Meaning: Mind your business if you are in someone's house. Do not tell them how to run their business unless your opinion is needed.

If you overlook a boiling pot, it will either overflow or burn.

Meaning: Address a problem before it gets worse.

African Village Man Kills Lion with a Pencil

My father always said, "Thank God no one is in charge of air. If someone was in charge of air, we would be in trouble, because some human beings are very difficult to deal with."

Meaning: Some people always think only about themselves. These people are called "me, myself, and I." If they are given the opportunity to rule the world, we would all be in trouble.

If I use $100 for the dentist, how much will that laugh be?

Meaning: The time and energy is sometimes not worth the cost.

My father also said that if you shoot a gun, he will not follow the bullet.

Meaning: If you try and try and give it your very best, do not pitch a fit.

An empty can makes the most noise.

Meaning: Some people who do not have much, or are not worth much, sometimes boast or brag about their wealth.

Victor Ekworomadu

Someone who is bitten by a snake is afraid of a worm.

Meaning: We should learn from our past mistakes and not repeat them.

It is always wise to take extra tissue when going to the bathroom in case of overflow.

Meaning: Always have a backup plan, a "plan A" and "plan B." If "plan A" fails, you have "plan B."

It is not proper to eat a gift and also eat thank you.

Meaning: Please say thank you if you receive a gift or a favor. Remember, the gift you were given was not an obligation.

If you offer a child candy and also offer another candy to his or her sibling, they will all be happy.

Meaning: In most cases, treat everyone fairly for peace and harmony.

The day you need a wife and go to the market to find one, that day the market will be filled with mad women.

Meaning: Things become scarce the day you need them.

No matter how good you are to a goat, it will still eat up your yam

Meaning: Some people will always be ungrateful no matter how helpful you are to them.

A roaring lion kills no game.

Meaning: Bragging or talking about your dreams alone can't make you achieve them.

Only a fool tests the depth of a river with both feet.

Meaning: Don't jump into a situation without first thinking about it.

Victor Ekworomadu

You don't teach the path of the forest to an old gorilla.

Meaning: The elders have more experience in this life, so we should learn to respect them and listen to their advice.

A restless foot may walk into a snake pit.

Meaning: A busybody or an idle person will always get into trouble if he is not careful.

He who swallows a complete coconut has absolute trust in his exit.

Meaning: Before making a crucial decision, you must make sure you have all it takes to bear the consequences.

Salt, sugar, and honey are very sweet. Despite being sweet, there has not been a time when you go to the store or market that you will not find them there.

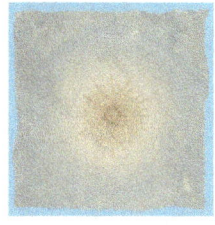

Meaning: Don't be so anxious or stressed out because of the materialism and fun of this world. Material things and fun things will always be available for you to enjoy.

An army of sheep led by a lion can defeat an army of lions led by a sheep.

Meaning: A good leader can lead even a group of incompetent people to success.

He who is brave enough can tell the lion his breath stinks.

Meaning: Some people will always be ungrateful no matter how helpful you are to them.

About the Author

Not only did the *African Village Man*, Victor Ekworomadu, *Kill a Lion with a Pencil*, he also strives to love **all people**, regardless of who they are, and is not influenced by the society or the world. He treats **all people** the way he wants to be treated, so when he looks back on his life, he won't have any regrets on how he treated his fellow human beings.

Hope and Love for Families of GA Inc.

Hope and Love is a 501 (c)(3) charitable nonprofit corporation in Georgia. FEIN: 65-1177111.
Hope and Love was formed to offer emergency assistance to families in need, especially the elderly, veterans, and women and children who need help due to circumstances beyond their control. Hope and Love also partners with and supports other nonprofit organizations that are in line with Hope and Love.
Your tax-deductible donation and purchase of this book will help Hope and Love kill many lions with a pencil.
With this "idiomatic expression," I mean help more families in our community.

For more information, please visit Hope and Love's website:
www.hopelove.org
Address: 2997 Cobb Parkway
Unit 723091
Atlanta, Georgia, 31139-0091
Contact: 770-649-9650, 404-667-5778
Email: hope@hopelove.org

www.ingramcontent.com/pod-product-compliance
Lightning Source LLC
Chambersburg PA
CBHW052145070526
44585CB00017B/1989